The True Story of Mass Avian Murder
and the Largest Surveillance Campaign
in US History

PETER McINDOE
AND
CONNOR GAYDOS

ST. MARTIN'S PRESS
NEW YORK

First published in the United States by St. Martin's Press, an imprint
of St. Martin's Publishing Group

www.stmartins.com

Designed by Omar Chapa

Images by Kris Finch

The Library of Congress Cataloging-in-Publication Data is available
upon request.

ISBN 978-1-250-28889-9 (hardcover)
ISBN 978-1-250-28890-5 (ebook)

Our books may be purchased in bulk for promotional, educational, or
business use. Please contact your local bookseller or the Macmillan
Corporate and Premium Sales Department at 1-800-221-7945, extension
5442, or by email at MacmillanSpecialMarkets@macmillan.com.

First Edition: 2024

10 9 8 7 6 5 4 3 2 1

This book is dedicated to the twelve billion innocent birds who perished at the hands of the United States government. Fly high, sweet angels.

CONTENTS

STOP

This book is intended for readers with an IQ over 250. Those are the only people with the intelligence required to comprehend the information within this text. If your IQ is under 250, please close this book immediately and read something more suited to your sensibilities, such as *Goodnight Moon* or *Frog and Toad*. Any classic children's book should do.

A NOTE FROM PETER McINDOE

What you're about to read is possibly the most dangerous book in the history of literature. I'm putting myself in great danger by writing it, and you are putting yourself in great danger by reading it. It's likely that you were added to some sort of government hit list the second you purchased the book. Welcome to the club. It's too late to turn back now, so you might as well continue.

For about six years now, I've been researching a massive government conspiracy. The story goes as follows: in the 1970s, **the United States government killed off the entire bird population and replaced them with robotic bird replicas that are used for mass surveillance.** Before I say any more about this, I'd like to take a minute to share what a devastating and dangerous journey this has been for me.

I am not the founder of the Birds Aren't Real movement. The movement began well over 40 years ago. There have been hundreds of brave patriots before me, ones who have done extensive research on this conspiracy and tried to stop it. Unfortunately, this original movement was brutally suppressed by the American government. By the time *I* heard about the obscure conspiracy theory colloquially known as "Birds Aren't Real," the movement was completely dead. I'm doing my best to pick up where the original Bird Truthers left off. To bring the fight against bird surveillance into the modern era.

In 2017, I began discussing my research on various Internet platforms and developed a small following. Almost immediately, the American government started to come after me. They had the official Birds Aren't Real website that I created taken down without explanation. My social media posts were constantly being flagged and removed. I was censored and shadowbanned on all platforms. They did everything they could to keep me from getting the truth out there. When I refused to remain silent, they took things to an extreme new level. They weren't just trying to silence me—they were trying to *take me out* completely.

I can't PROVE that the American government is trying to kill me, but what I *can* do is *accuse* them of it, and I would like to do that right now: I believe there have been many attempts by the government to secretly kill me. In August of 2018, for example, an air conditioner fell from a 15th-story window only three and a half miles from where I was walking. A few months later, I was served an undercooked hamburger at an Olive Garden restaurant. It's possible the cook just made a careless mistake, but it's also possible that even the Olive Garden has been compromised by the United States government.

These constant attempts on my life have sent me into hiding. I've been forced to vacate my home and relocate to an undisclosed location. I am still in hiding as I write this. Although I seem to be safe right now, it's very possible the government will find my secret hideout someday, and if they do, they might finally *finish the job*. Usually when the government takes out a target, they try to make it look like a suicide, so let me say this right now: I, Peter McIndoe, vow that I will never commit suicide under any circumstances whatsoever. If I am found dead in the near future and my death is ruled a suicide, *do not believe it*.

You may think that I'm just being paranoid, but to borrow a quote from the author Joseph Heller: "Just because you're paranoid doesn't mean they aren't after you." Perhaps Joseph Heller was onto something, because only 20 years after writing that quote, he died of Guillain-Barré syndrome.

Compiling all my information into this book is my last-ditch effort to end the government's bird surveillance project once and for all. As I've said, this is very dangerous, but I have to do what's right. All my life, I've had a recurring dream where the Founding Fathers appear before me and tell me that I have "an important battle to fight." I never knew what the dream meant until now. This is the battle they were talking about.

I hope you take this information seriously, and don't

just laugh it off like some naysayers on the Internet do. You might have some preconceived notions about "conspiracy theory." You might think it's all nonsense, and that everyone who buys into conspiracy theory is just some gullible deranged lunatic. If that's the case, I urge you to take a few hours to research the following topics: MKULTRA, COINTELPRO, the Gulf of Tonkin incident, Operation Northwoods, Moorer-Radford Affair, Operation Mockingbird, Special Collection Service, Operation Paperclip, MKOFTEN, Project ARTICHOKE, Operation Dormouse, the 1953 Iranian coup d'état, Project MERRIMAC, Stuxnet, Operation CHAOS, Project SHAMROCK, Operation Charly, Operation 40, Operation Midnight Climax, Operation Washtub, Acoustic Kitty, Stargate Project, Family Jewels, the Pentagon Papers, and Operation GLADIO.

Again, I implore you to look these topics up online. These are things that verifiably *did* happen. They are not conspiracy *theories,* they are conspiracy *facts.* They prove that the government does indeed *conspire* behind the scenes to do insane and illegal things.

Mind control. Torture. Unholy scientific experiments. False flags. Assassination attempts. Propaganda. Manipulation of the media. Coups d'état. Spying. These are all things the government has done, and they've done them in the shadows, without legal approval and without the consent of the people they're meant to represent. What else might they have done? What *wouldn't* they do?

If you're still reading at this point, you probably have a pretty open mind. I think you're ready. What follows is everything you need to know about bird surveillance and the Birds Aren't Real movement's efforts to stop it. I have scoured thousands of pages of leaked government documents, spoken to insiders, heard firsthand witness accounts, and experienced certain dreams and visions that I've chosen to interpret as divine wisdom. Everything you're about to read is 100% true. Once you learn it, you can't unlearn it. There is a burden that comes with that. More important, there's a *responsibility* that comes with it. It is your duty to spread this knowledge as much as you're able (you'll find some tips on how to raise awareness later in the book). Also, please be aware that once this book has been published, the government is going to attempt to confiscate and destroy every existing copy. It is your duty to keep your book safe! I suggest that you disassemble the book and laminate each individual page, then bury them in separate locations. Then, when you meet someone who is interested in learning more about our movement, unearth the pages, reassemble the book, and give it to the potential recruit to read.

If you're ready to take on that responsibility, please turn the page and continue reading. And please try to read this book very fast, otherwise they might kill you before you're able to finish it.

Godspeed, patriots.

1

WHAT DO YOU MEAN "BIRDS AREN'T REAL"?

When my fellow Bird Truthers and I say that birds aren't real, we don't mean that there's *no such thing* as birds. Of course birds are "real" creatures. There are billions of them out there right now, making the world a better place with their majestic beauty. *But NOT in the United States.*

In the 1970s, the Central Intelligence Agency systematically killed off the entire bird population in the United States. Ever since then, the birds have been replaced by billions of high-tech robotic drones that look and behave exactly like real birds. Later in this book you will read a thorough explanation of how and why the government eradicated the bird population, but for now, let's establish the most basic fact: if you're an American, **EVERY BIRD YOU HAVE EVER SEEN IN YOUR LIFE WAS ACTUALLY A ROBOTIC BIRD DRONE BUILT TO SPY ON YOU.** Bird drones are equipped with state-of-the-art cameras and microphones, allowing them to watch you closely and listen to everything you say, even in your own home.

This is what we mean when we say "birds aren't real." We mean the "birds" in America that populate our skies to this day are not actually living, breathing creatures at all. They are flying surveillance machines. "But Peter," you may be saying to yourself, "I don't live in America. I've never even *been* to America. Why should I care about any of this?" I'll tell you why: even as we speak, foreign governments around the world are trying to replicate the United States' bird surveillance program, and some of them are getting scarily close. China, for example, is about one year away from full-fledged bird surveillance. If you live in China, please translate this book into Chinese IMMEDIATELY so that you can save your country before it's too late!

I understand this is all terrifying information. Please try to stay calm. It is still possible to turn the tables on the government. But before we get into possible ways to fight back, you first need to understand how and why this happened . . .

2

OPERATION: WATER THE COUNTRY

People who are skeptical about bird surveillance tend to think it's simply impossible that the government could have gotten away with it. "There's no way they could have pulled off such a complicated operation!" they tell me. If only that were true. Even though our government leaders are mostly lazy and stupid, they were able to get away with killing off the birds because *we* are even stupider and even lazier. Let's explore the long and terrifying story of how and why the government committed mass bird genocide, launched the largest surveillance operation in history, and got away with it all unscathed.

THE BEGINNING

In the 1940s, a radical new political philosophy called communism was all the rage in the East. The communists dreamed of a classless society, one where the people would split everything and come together to build a shared utopia, **or else**. In Russia, communists were pulling once-powerful tsars from their thrones and beheading them in the streets. The American elites were terrified the same thing might happen in the United States. They decided it was necessary to keep a very close eye on the common people, to make sure they didn't develop any communist sympathies.

BIRTH OF THE CIA

So, the **CENTRAL INTELLIGENCE AGENCY** was created. The sole purpose of the CIA was to find a way to spy on as many American citizens as possible. The man in charge of this project was **ALLEN DULLES**. It was Dulles who originally conceived the idea of a bird surveillance program. It came to him as he was leaving the CIA offices after work one day. He arrived at his car in the parking lot, drunk, and discovered it had been defecated on by a bird. Dulles became enraged, remarking that he would "kill every last god damn bird on the planet" if he could. Just then, a radical idea came to him.

Allen Dulles's plan was simple in theory: the government would somehow kill off every bird in the country and replace them with flying surveillance robots disguised as birds. These flying bird drones would be the government's **eyes in the sky**. Dulles immediately brought this idea to **PRESIDENT DWIGHT D. EISEN-HOWER**. The president was intrigued, but wasn't exactly sure *how* the government would be able to pull it off. He told Dulles that if Dulles could figure out the logistics, he would approve the project and allocate billions of dollars to it.

THE PRESIDENTIAL SEAL OF APPROVAL

Dulles returned with a full written proposal a few days later. This proposal was vague and it didn't really address the question of how the federal government would implement the plan. Nevertheless, Eisenhower must have had faith that Dulles knew what he was doing, because he approved the proposal. The bird surveillance operation was now officially underway. Dulles and his CIA colleagues were given free rein to do whatever it took to get the project up and running. Their budget was virtually limitless. Eisenhower told his cabinet, "We must fund the bird surveillance project no matter what it takes. Take the money from the Department of Health and Human Services if we have to. Use the Department of Education like a piggy bank—I don't care!" With the President's blessing, Dulles got to work on bringing the bird surveillance program to life.

Opposite: Allen Dulles's proposal for a bird surveillance program

MEMORANDUM FROM: Allen Dulles, Director for Central Intelligence Service
TO: President Dwight D. Eisenhower
SUBJECT: Proposal for Avian Surveillance Project

APPROVED

Mr. President,

You already know it is in the country's best interest that the federal government take bigger steps to prevent the spread of communism. Sweeping surveillance measures are required to do so. The Central Intelligence proposes a secret operation in which 100% of the bird population is eliminated over the course of a few years and replaced with state-of-the-art surveillance drones disguised to look like birds. These robot bird replicas would be equipped with powerful cameras and microphones. With billions of these bird replicas in circulation the federal government would have "eyes and ears" on every inch of the country.

I have already shared with you my original concept drawing for this operation. You expressed the need for more information on the logistics of the plan. All your logistical questions are answered here.

1. BY WHAT MEANS WILL THE BIRD POPULATION BE KILLED OFF?
   Excellent question.

2. DOES THE TECHNOLOGY FOR THE BIRD-ROBOTS ALREADY EXIST, AND IF NOT, WHICH ENTITY OR ENTITIES WILL BE RESPONSIBLE FOR DEVELOPING IT?
   No, the technology does not yet exist.

3. WHAT MEASURES WILL BE TAKEN TO ENSURE THAT THE PROJECT REMAINS A SECRET FROM BOTH THE AMERICAN PUBLIC AND FOREIGN GOVERNMENTS OVERSEAS?
   Yes.

4. HOW MUCH IS THE FEDERAL GOVERNMENT PROJECTED TO SPEND ON THE PROJECT?
   Several billion dollars.

5. FROM START TO FINISH HOW LONG WILL IT TAKE THE FEDERAL GOVERNMENT TO REPLACE 100% OF THE BIRD POPULATION WITH SURVEILLANCE ROBOTS?
   Correct.

POISON THE SKY

The first step was to figure out how to kill off every bird in the country. Dulles believed the most efficient way would be to poison the bird population en masse using customized military planes. These planes would fly undetected in the night sky, raining down a specialized poison that would kill the birds without hurting any other living creature. The problem was that no such poison existed. It would need to be invented, and fast.

Luckily, the CIA had been researching and developing different poisons for many years. It was one of the many methods they used to secretly take out foreign enemies. In fact, there was an entire department at the CIA dedicated to developing new poisons. One morning in 1957, Allen Dulles burst into the Poison Department and demanded to speak to the "main guy." He ordered the department head to start working on a specialized poison that only affected birds. He also needed the poison to make the bird corpses decompose quickly, because it would arouse suspicion if billions of dead birds were suddenly littering the country. The Poison Department quietly got to work on developing this specialized poison. It was finished a year later. Lab tests showed it was 100% effective in killing birds, and it had no effect on any other living life-forms. It also caused the corpses of the birds to decompose within 20 minutes, on average.

BOEING ONCE, BOEING TWICE . . .

Next, it was time to find planes suitable for this poison-dumping operation. **THE BOEING COMPANY** had been building planes for the American military for years, so Dulles went to them first. It was in May of 1957 that Dulles met with an unidentified engineer from Boeing and ordered him to oversee the building of 120 specialized B-52 bombers for a top-secret bird killing operation. When the Boeing engineer began asking too many questions, Dulles told him, "This is none of your business, junior. Just build the planes, or I'll have to introduce you to Old Trusty." Old Trusty was the name of a wrench that Allen Dulles often used to threaten people who questioned him. He once described Old Trusty as "the most influential figure in American politics." Fears of being hit by a huge wrench haunted the Boeing engineer's mind as he reluctantly agreed to take on the task of designing the 120 specialized B-52 bombers.

The building of the planes had to be kept top-secret. The American public would be outraged if they knew how much money was being spent on this domestic surveillance operation. This project would require at least 20 engineers. That was a lot of mouths to be kept shut, and Dulles only had one wrench. So, Dulles vetted the engineers carefully. He wanted to hire engineers who had no family and no friends, so that they would have no one to squeal to about the project. Dulles conducted interviews with over 100 engineers, trying to find the biggest "losers" he could. Each interview was recorded on cassette tape. An early patriot of the Birds Aren't Real movement managed to steal a box of these tapes from an undisclosed warehouse in the state of Nevada. A partial transcript of one of these tapes follows below.

ALLEN DULLES
I see on your resume that you went to the Massachusetts Institute of Technology.

BOEING ENGINEER
Yes, sir.

ALLEN DULLES

That's a great school and all, but let me ask you a question, junior. Do you know how to keep your mouth shut?

BOEING ENGINEER

Pardon?

ALLEN DULLES

Do you know how to keep your mouth shut? Keep that little clap-trap of yours closed real tight?

BOEING ENGINEER

Uh . . . yes, sir.

ALLEN DULLES

How about your personal life? Do you have any family?

BOEING ENGINEER

No, sir. I'm single, no children.

ALLEN DULLES

Any siblings? Parents?

BOEING ENGINEER

No, sir. I have no siblings, and my parents are no longer with us. My father passed away just last month.

ALLEN DULLES
Awesome.

BOEING ENGINEER
What?

ALLEN DULLES
Nothing. So what do you do for fun?

BOEING ENGINEER
I'm not sure. I work a lot, so . . .

ALLEN DULLES
So you don't have much of a social life?

BOEING ENGINEER
No, I suppose not.

ALLEN DULLES
No friends?

BOEING ENGINEER
No, not really.

(Unintelligible noise, possibly a sniffle from the engineer)

ALLEN DULLES
Last question: have you ever been hit in the head
with a huge wrench?

BOEING ENGINEER

No.

ALLEN DULLES

Would you *like* to be?

BOEING ENGINEER

What?

ALLEN DULLES

Would you like to be hit in the head with a huge wrench?

BOEING ENGINEER

No, of course not, sir.

ALLEN DULLES

Great. You seem qualified. You're hired.

After hundreds of these interviews, Allen Dulles selected 23 Boeing engineers for the project. In a progress report to the president, Dulles said: "I have vetted our engineers carefully, and I'm confident they won't tell anyone about the project. Even if they wanted to squeal about the project, they have no one to tell. We're talking total, A-grade losers with no family or friends. Just a dogshit group of guys."

Still, there was potential for leaks. This was a massive operation that required a lot of space, and it would be difficult to carry out the building of the planes without the public seeing. Boeing headquarters was in Seattle, where there were millions of potential witnesses. It would be too risky to build the planes there. They needed to set up shop somewhere remote. The CIA knew just the place . . .

AREA 51 OR BUST

The CIA conspired to relocate the Boeing engineers to **AREA 51**, where there was zero chance any civilians would see them coming and going. This is where the planes would be built. Motivated by a lack of respect and a desire to save money, Dulles told the Boeing engineers that they were responsible for arranging their own travel to Area 51. This was a big mistake.

Dulles's strategy of selecting "loners" for the project backfired. These engineers ended up really hitting it off. These lonely men bonded over their love of aeronautics, and even further bonded over their shared involvement in a top-secret project. To them it felt like a party—the first one they were ever invited to. It was all very thrilling.

Furthermore, because they were not the most socially adept people, Allen Dulles's veiled threats went over their heads. We're talking about grown men with absolutely zero social awareness. He had strongly hinted to them that they needed to stay quiet about the project, or *else*. The engineers didn't quite pick up on the hint, and they ended up drawing quite a bit of attention to themselves.

The 23 engineers, now best friends, decided to carpool together from Seattle to Area 51. They all pitched in and bought an old bus from a salvage yard in Mukilteo, Washington. They made their destination very clear.

The Boeing engineers treated the three-day drive to Area 51 like a road trip. They spray-painted "Area 51 or Bust" on the side of the bus, and started calling themselves "The 23 Busketeers." They were happy to answer any questions that people asked them along the way. It's estimated they told upwards of 30 people what they were up to.

They could not have been less discreet. When they would stop for breaks at rest stops along the way, they would break out guitars and sing songs with titles such as "I Left My Honey for Area 51," "Hey Hey, Let's Kill the Birds," and "We Are Driving to Area 51 Because We Have Been Hired to Construct Secret Planes for the Government" (this one was the worst in terms of melody). They were quite simply having the time of their lives.

However, there was one engineer who did not make it to Nevada. This man's name was **MIKE WAZOWSKI**. The other engineers found Mike annoying. He needed to stop for bathroom breaks too frequently, and he was constantly asking the other engineers if they liked him. The consensus on Mike was that he was killing the vibe of the road trip. The others began conspiring to "lose" him. They ended up leaving him behind in a Waffle House bathroom somewhere outside of Boise, Idaho.

WHO WAS MIKE WAZOWSKI?

Mike Wazowski is the reason that we know so much about Boeing's involvement in the bird elimination operation today. He blew the whistle on the whole thing shortly after the Waffle House fiasco. In a diary entry, he wrote of the incident: "For the first time in my life, I finally had friends. I thought we were having a great road trip. But for me, the road ended at the bathroom of the Waffle House, and so did my hopes for human connection."

THE BOEING B-52B BOMBER

Meanwhile, the rest of the engineers arrived safely at Area 51, where they began work on the specialized B-52 planes. As instructed, they made several modifications to Boeing's classic B-52 design. Instead of bomb compartments on the underside of the plane, there were 450-gallon water tanks, where the bird poison could be stored. Each plane was equipped with a sophisticated radar system, used for tracking large flocks of birds. The planes were also sprayed with several coats of jet-black paint so they would not be seen in the night sky. No lights of any kind were built into the planes—no strobes, beacons, or landing lights. The Pratt & Whitney JT3D engines were equipped with noise reduction technology, so that the planes would not make a sound and draw unwanted attention. These cutting-edge aircraft became known as **B-52Bs** and soon they would take to the skies to carry out their genocidal mission.

In the span of about two years, the Boeing engineers had completed 120 bombers exactly as instructed. The CIA considered it a massive success. The engineers, however, would look back on this time as a grueling slog through hell. An early patriot of the Birds Aren't Real movement named Eugene Price (much more on him later) managed to steal 12 pallets of classified CIA documents that shed light on the harsh working conditions these engineers had to endure. They were forced to work shifts up to 15 hours long with very little food or water. The work was done in a windowless, non-air-conditioned space (there *were* air conditioners in the facilities, but Allen Dulles said they weren't allowed to use them). A few engineers tried to speak up about the horrible conditions, but this only aroused Allen Dulles's anger. He would threaten them with Old Trusty, or, in more extreme cases, threaten to have them drafted to fight in the Laotian Civil War.

In fact, Allen Dulles *often* threatened to send people to war. According to a former assistant of his, Dulles later tried to have a 16-year-old busboy sent to Vietnam after the busboy spilled a small amount of oatmeal on Dulles's shoe at a diner. When Dulles's assistant informed him that the busboy was too young to be drafted, Dulles got angry and yelled, "Well, *someone* has to go to 'Nam!" Dulles then quietly arranged for his assistant, whose name was Tex, to be sent to Vietnam instead. This is the same Tex who was portrayed in the hit 1993 film *Forrest Gump*.

CENTRAL INTELLIGENCE AGENCY

MEMORANDUM

From: Allen Dulles, Director for the Central Intelligence Service

To: Office of the U.S. Selective Service System

Subj: Send Kevin to Nam

Please send my assistant, Kevin "Tex" Finnerty, to Vietnam immediately.

Thank you,

The planes were built, but Dulles did not trust the Boeing engineers to keep quiet. They had already attracted a lot of attention during their Seattle-to-Nevada road trip. In order to tie up these loose ends, Dulles decided to "do to them what I did to Tex." He quietly arranged for all 23 Boeing engineers to be sent to the front lines of battle in Vietnam. None of them made it back. Perhaps they're out there in the stars somewhere, laughing and singing their little songs.

On June 2nd, 1959, the B-52B planes took to the skies and began the long process of poisoning the bird population. The most ambitious surveillance operation in the history of human civilization, which had been named **OPERATION: WATER THE COUNTRY**, was now well underway.

However, the CIA would soon face an unforeseen hurdle: pushback from the top of the federal government itself. This pushback came from a handsome, bright young Catholic man by the name of **JOHN F. KENNEDY**.

THE KENNEDY PROBLEM

Kennedy took the presidency after Eisenhower and immediately began to realize there were huge decisions being made without his express approval. He heard stories of the CIA experimenting with mind control (MK-ULTRA), staging overseas coups d'état (Guatemala), and sabotaging civil rights groups (COINTELPRO). He did not understand how or why the CIA had so much power. In fact, Kennedy hardly understood why the CIA existed at *all*. Its purpose was almost completely unclear to him. We can see his frustration and confusion in an exchange he had with CIA director Allen Dulles in 1961.

The CIA were immediately frustrated with their new president. He was asking too many questions. A culture of hating JFK became pervasive. They referred to him as "The Narc," and plastered pictures of his face on dartboards and urinals at CIA headquarters. At office parties, CIA agents would beat Kennedy-shaped piñatas with clubs. Irish Catholic jokes were told constantly. And sometimes, they'd even joke about how easy it would be to assassinate Kennedy. Allen Dulles allegedly once joked, "With a head *that* big, you couldn't miss."

All the while, they continued to carry out their secret operations without the president's knowledge. Kennedy had absolutely no idea what was being done to the birds. At least not at first. But he would soon become *well* aware of the existence of Operation: Water the Country. How? By doing a little surveillance of his own.

Throughout his first year as president, Kennedy's lunch would mysteriously go missing from the White House fridge on a daily basis. The first few times it happened he believed it was an honest mistake, but when it kept happening, he started to suspect foul play. He believed the CIA was behind the repeated sandwich theft. He knew they hated him—stealing his lunch was exactly the type of prank they would pull. To confirm his

THE WHITE HOUSE

WASHINGTON

April 19, 1961

MEMORANDUM TO: CIA Director Allen Dulles
FROM: President John F. Kennedy
SUBJECT: What is the CIA

Mr. Dulles,
Would you mind telling me what in the name of
Christ you people even do?

Regards,

CENTRAL INTELLIGENCE AGENCY

VIRGINIA

April 25, 1961

MEMORANDUM TO: PRESIDENT JOHN F. KENNEDY
FROM: CIA Director Allen Dulles
SUBJECT: RE: What do we even do

Mr. Kennedy,
We do a number of things, and not one of them is
your business. Go fiddle around with your little
space program and leave the big things to us.

Regards,

suspicions, he tapped the phones of every single person at the CIA and began listening to their conversations.

One of the phones that Kennedy wiretapped was that of Alvin B. Cleaver, who was the Internal Communications Director for the CIA at the time. In 1963, Kennedy listened in on a phone call between Cleaver and Allen Dulles. This call was the smoking gun that confirmed Cleaver was the sandwich thief. But it also confirmed something else: the existence of a secret plot to replace all the birds with surveillance robots. In the Bird Truther community, we refer to this call as **THE BIG ONE**. A partial transcript is reproduced below.

ALLEN DULLES
Cleaver, you son of a bitch, how are ya?

ALVIN B. CLEAVER
Very well, sir.

ALLEN DULLES
Hey, I got a joke for you. How do Irish Catholics get into heaven?

ALVIN B. CLEAVER
How?

ALLEN DULLES
They just wait for the bar to open!

ALVIN B. CLEAVER

(Laughter)

Oh man, that's good. I'd love to
hear what the president thinks of
that one. That idiot. Speaking of
which, you'll get a kick out of this.
I've been stealing his ham sandwich from the White House fridge
every day for about a year now.

ALLEN DULLES

(Laughter)

Oh yeah?

ALVIN B. CLEAVER

Yeah. You should see him. He's
walking around like, "Where in
the name of sweet Christ is my
ham sandwich?"

ALLEN DULLES

(Laughter)

Oh man.

ALVIN B. CLEAVER

I've never seen the guy so pissed.
You should see his face. It's as
red as a baboon's ass.

ALLEN DULLES

(Laughter)

ALVIN B. CLEAVER

I'm thinking I'll keep stealing
his sandwiches until he launches
a full-fledged investigation.
Then, after I've stolen, like, a
hundred of them, I'm going to
dump them *all* on his desk one
day. Just an absolute mountain
of rotting ham and moldy
Wonder Bread in the middle of
the Resolute desk.

ALLEN DULLES

(Laughter)

He'll be like, "What the hell!?"

(More laughter)

Anyway, listen, I was just calling
to check in on Operation:
Water the Country. How are things
proceeding?

ALVIN B. CLEAVER

Excellent, sir. We've eliminated
about 220 million birds so far.

ALLEN DULLES

How about the drones? Where are we at with the
switcheroo?

ALVIN B. CLEAVER

The bird drones are being built
as we speak, sir.

ALLEN DULLES

And the president still has no idea?

ALVIN B. CLEAVER

Nope. He's completely in the
dark on this.

ALLEN DULLES

What an idiot.

ALVIN B. CLEAVER

(Laughter)

Yep.

Kennedy was infuriated by the call. The CIA had
made a fool of him, and they were laughing about it

behind his back. He ordered Dulles and Cleaver into his office and demanded that the CIA discontinue the bird surveillance program immediately. But that was not going to happen.

Non-murderer Lee Harvey Oswald

How did President John F. Kennedy die? You were probably taught that he was assassinated by a lone gunman, Lee Harvey Oswald, while riding through Dallas in the presidential motorcade. This "official" narrative behind JFK's death is absurd nonsense that does not hold up to even the slightest bit of scrutiny. Lee Harvey Oswald did not shoot and kill John F. Kennedy. Nobody did. No *person,* at least.

THE JFK ASSASSINATION

As you'll soon learn in the Bird Drone Field Guide, most bird drones are built strictly for surveillance, but there are a few models that are designed for more specific tasks. One of these specialty models is the **HUMMINGBIRD DRONE**, which is designed to kill. When the American government needs to take out a human target quickly and discreetly, nothing gets the job done quite like a hummingbird drone.

The CIA was not willing to take orders from the president. When Dulles and Cleaver were ordered to discontinue the bird surveillance operation, it was time for them to start discussing the "nuclear option." By that I mean they literally discussed dropping a nuclear bomb on John F. Kennedy, but after realizing that that would be too conspicuous, they decided to "send in the Hummingbird" instead.

The Zapruder film, which I would consider one of my least favorite films of all time, has been dissected by conspiracy theorists for decades. Almost all of them agree that it depicts JFK being assassinated in the back of a limousine, but beyond that, they are fiercely divided on the facts of what *really* happened that day. After years of careful examination, Birds Aren't Real activists have discovered a few frames of the Zapruder film that seem to show the presence of a small, dark "speck" hovering near the motorcade at the exact moment the kill shot was fired. Because the film is so old and worn out, it is difficult to enhance. But to many of us in the community, that mysterious speck sure looks a lot like a CIA hummingbird drone.

Throughout the years, there have been hundreds of theories about what *really* happened in Dealey Plaza that day. Some of these theories sound plausible. Many of them do not. In all my years of research, I have yet to find a theory more plausible than the hummingbird drone theory. It is my belief that the CIA used a hummingbird drone to shoot and kill John F. Kennedy, then used Lee Harvey Oswald as a patsy to take the fall.

In 1963, the government launched a full investigation into the strange circumstances of Kennedy's assassination. This was called the Warren Commission. It was the Warren Commission that pushed the preposterous lone gunman narrative. Their "evidence" for the lone gunman theory has been refuted extensively by forensic scientists, firearms experts, physicists, YouTube videos of men yelling at their phones inside of trucks, and a whole slew of independent researchers. I'd like to encourage you to do a little research of your own. Specifically, look up *who* was on the Warren Commission. One name might sound familiar to you: **Allen Dulles.**

THE TRUE STORY OF VIETNAM

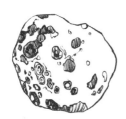

Bauxite

The Kennedy problem was solved, but another problem soon arose. Construction of the bird drones required a plentiful amount of **BAUXITE**, a clayey, amorphous rock that is the chief commercial core of aluminum. There was not nearly enough bauxite in the West to build the bird drones. However, there *was* a rich surplus of bauxite in **VIETNAM**.

You were probably taught that the US went into Vietnam to help stop a communist revolution in the North. Once again, you've been lied to. The American government always knew that trying to topple the communist regime led by Ho Chi Minh would be futile. President Lyndon B. Johnson himself once remarked, "If we send soldiers into Vietnam, Ho Chi Minh is going to turn them into Ho Chi mincemeat." The war was never about thwarting the Viet Cong. The US entered the war for the same reason it entered so many other wars: the pursuit of precious resources.

On July 2nd, 1964, members of the CIA met with a group of high-ranking military officials in the Jefferson Building in Washington, DC. On that day, a generation-defining decision was made: we would officially join the war under the pretext of fighting communism, but *really,* we would be going to extract bauxite in North Vietnam.

Vietnam recruitment poster

Lyndon B. Johnson, who became president after JFK was shot to death by a hummingbird drone, fully supported this plan. He loved Operation: Water the Country and was willing to send millions of American troops overseas to help. In a secret meeting with the CIA that spring, he said, "If a thousand American soldiers must die for a single handful of rock, then so be it."

The government fired up the propaganda machine once again, urging every able-bodied American to enlist to fight in the war. Additionally, over two million American men were drafted. Very few of them had any idea why they were *really* there. They thought they were there to stop a brutal communist uprising in the North, because that's what they (and all the rest of us) were told. While thousands of American soldiers were engaging in violent warfare with the North Vietnamese, a separate, carefully vetted faction of soldiers was off digging up bauxite. These soldiers, who were told by the CIA that they were "the real heroes of the Vietnam War," would fortify small perimeters of land in North Vietnam that were rich in bauxite. Once flanking defenses were set up, dozens of excavators would be brought in to dig up the bauxite and load it into dump trucks for delivery to the United States.

The CIA celebrates "victory" in Vietnam

ATOMIC AMERICA

With the bauxite secured, there were only a few more logistical hurdles to face before Operation: Water the Country could take off. The CIA needed to find a place where the bird drones could be built in secret, and an entire staff of people to build them. People who wouldn't *talk*. The original plan was to build the bird drones at Area 51, the same place they had built the B-52B planes. But the personnel at Area 51 wanted nothing more to do with Operation: Water the Country. They had grown annoyed by Allen Dulles. He was constantly stopping by Area 51, micromanaging the personnel, and repeatedly demanding to "see one of the aliens."

The only option was to construct *new* facilities where the bird drones could be built. The CIA's first idea was to have caves throughout the United States hollowed out. The first bird drone manufacturing facilities were built inside these hollowed-out caves, but they frequently collapsed, injuring the technicians and damaging the precious bird drones. It was an unsafe, unsustainable way of doing things. So, a new plan was hatched: the bird drones would be built in subterranean bunkers disguised as nuclear fallout shelters. Now we get into the *real* story of the **COLD WAR**.

Ever since President Truman dropped the atomic bomb on Japan in 1945, Americans wondered when it would be our turn. Nuclear anxiety was the new reality. For the shadow government, that was a good thing, because fear can be exploited and used to justify extreme government overreach. In this case, it could be used to justify the sudden influx of nuclear fallout shelters across the country, which would *actually* be used as bird drone manufacturing facilities.

An American schoolchild practices the futile
"duck and cover" maneuver.

So, the US began drumming up as much nuclear anxiety as possible. The media (much of which was/is controlled by the shadow government) became saturated with nuclear terror. Stories about the Soviets' growing nuclear arsenal ran on the news every single night. CIA-owned newspapers spread wild exaggerations, even claiming that the Soviets had "an entire nuclear bomb for every one American." Even the youth weren't spared from the propaganda. Public Service Announcements taught children the "duck and cover" maneuver, telling them that they should drop to the floor and take cover under a desk in the event of a nuclear bombing. Teachers and children participated in "duck and cover" drills at school, foolishly believing that two inches of wood could protect them from a nuclear blast.

It was a terrifying time to be alive in America. Thus, the shadow government had the excuse it needed to construct as many massive underground facilities as needed, as long as they marked them as "fallout shelters." There were 22 of these shelters spread out across the States, with hundreds of technicians building bird drones around the clock.

But who, exactly, were these technicians? How could so many people willingly participate in such a cruel project? Why have none of them spoken out, even decades later? The truth is that they didn't even know what they were doing down there themselves. Why not? Because they were absolutely *tripping balls.*

ACID CHRONICLES

The sixties were a crazy time in America. All the societal unease of the previous decades gave birth to the "hippie

revolution." The hippies were young, free-spirited liberals who detested the violence that was going on overseas in Vietnam. These idealistic young people believed the only way to stop violence was through radical acts of peace, love, and self-indulgence. The general idea was that if they did enough drugs and had enough dirty sex outdoors, the government would end the Vietnam War, for some reason. It didn't work.

In fact, the hippies were an *asset* to the American government. The hippie revolution was very easy to exploit. And it was crucial to the bird surveillance project.

The hippies took a lot of drugs. They would often say "the most powerful drug of all is *love*," but it's actually **LYSERGIC ACID DIETHYLAMIDE**. LSD, or "acid," is a powerful psychedelic drug that causes the user to experience feelings of euphoria, *hopefully*. It can just as easily induce hellish feelings of doom and dread that never go away for the rest of your life. Nevertheless, the hippies took that gamble over and over again, consuming heroic amounts of acid throughout the sixties and seventies. Many popular countercultural icons were advocates of the drug, including Grateful Dead frontman Jerry Garcia, author William S. Burroughs, and aspiring folk musician Charles Manson.

The CIA became very interested in the drug. They conducted a number of bizarre experiments involving LSD, none of which seemed to result in anything scientifically significant. Still, their interest in the drug persisted. It seemed very possible that LSD could help them achieve a goal they'd had for a long time: human mind control.

THE HORRIFIC STORY OF "MKULTRA"

At this time, many scientists thought that mind control was theoretically possible. They began researching mind control techniques under a top-secret program called MKULTRA. The MKULTRA program used nonconsenting human beings as guinea pigs in a variety of bizarre experiments. Captured Soviet spies were among the first people to be experimented on. CIA-funded scientists would feed the Soviet spies psychoactive drugs, then attempt to put them under hypnosis. In their psychedelic, hypnotic state, they'd be urged to confess to their crimes, disavow their Soviet ideals, and pledge their devotion to the West. Essentially the CIA was trying to wipe their brains clean and reprogram them completely.

Soviet POWs were not the only people to be used as guinea pigs. There were plenty of vulnerable citizens right here on our own soil who were ripe for nonconsensual scientific experimentation. Prisoners, mental patients, prostitutes, and even veterans were targeted and used as MKULTRA test subjects.

MKULTRA was not only illegal and inhumane, it was also a failure. The CIA ultimately determined that mind control is not possible, no matter how much LSD you feed to a person. As powerful as the drug is, it cannot "wipe one's brain clean, thus allowing it to be utterly reprogrammed from scratch" like the CIA had hoped. However, taking a lot of acid *can* make you pretty dumb, and dumbness is easy to exploit. That's how the CIA

CENTRAL INTELLIGENCE AGENCY

3 AUGUST 1965

MEMORANDUM FROM: Allen Dulles, Director for Central Intelligence Service
TO: President Dwight D. Eisenhower
SUBJECT: Proposal for an internal scientific experiment to better understand the effects of the hallucinogenic drug known as lysergic acid diethylamide

We want to give LSD to an elephant and see what happens.

Signed,

APPROVED

The CIA conducted a number of bizarre experiments in the sixties to better understand the effects of LSD.

CENTRAL INTELLIGENCE AGENCY

MEMORANDUM

FROM: Allen Dulles, Director for the Central Intelligence Service

TO: CIA MKULTRA team

SUBJECT: Round up the cattle!

Team,

We will be moving forward with the mind control program. In order to determine whether LSD can be used to rewrite the human mind we will need a number of test subjects. It has been determined that the best subjects would be people among the "lower ranks" of society i.e. people whose reputations are questionable and who have virtually no support system in their lives. Ideal candidates include prisoners, prostitutes, johns, druggies, lunatics, veterans, and general low lives. People no one would miss. We'll hold off on children for now but down the line I'd like to at least open it up for discussion. We'll be meeting this Monday to discuss our strategy for finding these subjects, then we can get rockin' and rollin' on this.

Respectfully,

[signature]

With the MKULTRA program, the CIA began testing the effects of acid on unwitting test subjects.

managed to turn the hippies of the 1960s into unwitting, unpaid drone technicians.

At some point in 1969, the CIA met to discuss how they would assemble their team of drone technicians. Hundreds of workers were needed for the task, and it would be difficult to keep them all quiet. It would also be very expensive to pay them all, and Dulles was very close to blowing the massive budget he'd been given (he'd allegedly spent a third of the multibillion-dollar budget on personal items, including meals, suits, and an indoor hot tub for his office). In their internal 1969 meeting, he remarked to his peers: "Ideally, we would get people to build the bird drones without them even realizing what they were doing. And if we could do it all without paying them, that would really be spectacular. There's got to be a way to pull this off . . . I'm going to hit the hot tub and stew on this for a while."

A dripping wet Allen Dulles emerged from the hot tub hours later with an idea: he would use the hippies. He'd had many run-ins with the local hippies in Virginia and deeply despised them. Large groups of them would often assemble outside CIA headquarters and sing protest songs urging the government to stop the Vietnam War (it did not work). During the March on the Pentagon of 1967, a large group of hippies attempted to use their psychic energy to make the Pentagon levitate into the sky. This didn't work either, but Dulles was still pretty mad they tried.

He hated the hippies more than anything. When he

would leave the office at the end of the workday, they would follow him to the parking lot, berate him, and spit on his car. He was disgusted by the hippie movement, and he always dreamed of putting them in their place somehow. His new plan would kill two birds with one stone. It would get the bird drones built *and* make fools of the hippies at the same time.

A TOP-SECRET "PEACEKEEPING" MISSION

The plan went as follows: undercover government agents disguised as hippies would recruit actual hippies for a "peacekeeping mission." The hippies were told they'd be helping assemble bird robots, which would be used to fly supplies into Vietnam for the innocent civilians. They would build these helpful bird robots in a "groovy underground shelter" so that this peacekeeping mission would remain a secret from the oppressive American government.

In reality, they would be building the American government's secret surveillance robots without even realizing it. They'd be fed an endless supply of LSD, which would keep them too dumb and docile to question any of it. And if they told anyone about what they were doing down there, it would sound like the deranged ramblings of a brain-dead psychonaut.

The plan was as ambitious as it was absurd, but against all odds, it worked. Across the country, undercover government agents disguised as hippies successfully infiltrated music festivals, protests, and other

Senior drone assembly technicians

hippie-friendly events. They invited thousands of hippies to come help build the "peace birds," promising them a plentiful supply of psychedelic drugs down there in the bunkers. Within months, the CIA had recruited upwards of 15,000 "workers" to assemble the drones. Behind closed doors, Allen Dulles and his CIA buddies laughed uproariously at what they had accomplished. They had turned the peaceniks—who detested the government—into unpaid government workers. "That'll teach them to spit on my car," remarked Allen Dulles.

THE GREAT PUMPKINHEAD OUTBREAK

DISCLAIMER:

The following content is extremely disturbing. If you have a weak stomach, please skip this section and proceed to pg. 49.

Although the CIA's special bird poison was nonlethal to humans, it did cause some people to develop a disgusting and bizarre new medical condition known as "pumpkinhead." Victims of pumpkinhead would develop a severe rash on their face and head. Over time the rash would cause their skin to develop a permanent orange hue. Pumpkinhead also causes the human head to swell up to five times its normal size. It's estimated that about 250 Americans developed the condition as a result of breathing the CIA's experimental bird poison.

One victim of pumpkinhead was a young woman from Bartlesville, Oklahoma, named Laura K. In the early 1960s, Laura was a happy and healthy teenage girl. She was both a straight-A student and the junior prom queen at Bartlesville High. She had her whole life ahead of her, and the future was looking bright. Then one day in 1962, she woke up and nearly fainted when she looked into the bathroom mirror. Her head was suddenly the size and color of a ripe pumpkin. Her parents rushed her to the local hospital, where she was examined by a slew of doctors. None of them had any idea what they were looking at. Laura and her parents spent the next year reaching out to various specialists throughout the United States, but none of them could help. Finally, Laura's mother decided to contact the local news station, hoping that they would take an interest in Laura's story. They thought that if they could get Laura on TV, maybe someone out there would be able to offer some answers. One morning news show called *Good Morning, Bartlesville!* agreed to have Laura on. Days later, Laura made her only public appearance. Studio lights shined brightly upon her revolting gourd as she stared pleadingly into the camera and urged the viewers to reach out if they had any answers.

Four years ago, a Birds Aren't Real activist who wishes to remain anonymous named Kurt Fetter broke

Laura K., pumpkinhead survivor

into the studio where *Good Morning, Bartlesville!* is filmed, and managed to steal the original film reel containing Laura's appearance on the show. He digitized the film and uploaded it online to share with the Birds Aren't Real community, but the video has since been scrubbed from the Internet (once again, we can only assume this was a cleanup job by the CIA). I am one of the few people who managed to watch the clip before it was suppressed. I was as deeply moved by Laura's heartfelt message as I was deeply nauseated by the sight of her sickening pumpkin-tinted noggin.

But one person who was not moved to tears was Allen Dulles at the CIA. In an internal memo (which has unfortunately been lost), he said: "Some broad in Horsefuck, Oklahoma, is starting to squawk about pumpkinhead. We need to take care of this before she gets the word out."

Four days after Laura's appearance on local television, she was contacted by a man claiming to be a doctor. He went by the name of Dr. Niceman. The "doctor" told Laura he was a "specialist in non-communicable diseases" and had been researching pumpkinhead for many months. He invited her to visit his office in Kansas City. Laura accepted the invitation. She was so thrilled to finally have someone who could help. A "medical van" was sent to Laura's farmhouse to pick her up and transport her to Dr. Niceman's office. The van arrived at roughly 9:18 a.m. on August 18th, 1967. Laura got in. This was the last time anyone ever saw her. Laura's parents, Janet and Christian, who also had pumpkinhead,

Janet and Christian Duffy

spent the rest of their lives trying to figure out what happened on that fateful day, but they never did. They also spent years trying to figure out what caused their sudden health condition. They didn't have any luck with that, either. It was only recently that we Bird Truthers figured out that pumpkinhead was caused by the CIA's bird poison.

By now, you have a thorough understanding of how and why the government did all this. You're probably fuming with rage, anxiously pacing around your home, punching holes in the drywall. I know *I* am. I've had to take several "punch breaks" over the course of writing this—the walls of my hideout look like Swiss cheese at this point. You are probably ready to *take action*. So, enough of the history lesson—it's time to start discussing how we Bird Truthers can actually fight back. The first step toward fighting back against bird drones is learning about how they work, and how to identify them . . .

3

BIRD DRONE FIELD GUIDE

*If you know the enemy and know yourself, you
need not fear the result of a hundred battles. If
you know yourself but not the enemy, for every
victory gained you will also suffer a defeat. If
you know neither the enemy nor yourself, you
will succumb in every battle.*

—SUN TZU, *THE ART OF WAR*

Contrary to popular belief, surveillance is not the only
application for bird drones. Yes, surveillance is their *primary* function, but the government would never waste an
opportunity to milk these robotic replicas for all they're
worth. Certain bird drones are designed for specific purposes aside from keeping an eye on the public.

What follows is something I wish I had been given
when I first discovered the truth: a Bird Drone Field
Guide. This was designed to help you better identify and

understand some of the bird drones that surround you in your everyday life.

You cannot beat bird surveillance until you've learned how to *recognize* it. How it *works*. Knowledge is a weapon. This book is essentially an atomic bomb. So, please familiarize yourself with the following guide, memorize it, and brand it into your psyche. Some Bird Truthers have been known to tattoo the guide on their forearms.

Do you have a copier or printer in your home? Consider pressing the following pages onto the scanner, and handing out prints to people around your community. Tell them it's for their own good, even if they don't know it yet. They will love it and thank you, as long as they are smart, high-IQ members of society. If they aren't, you should not be associating with them anyway—cease all contact with them immediately. As they say, you are the company you keep!

Without further ado, here is the official *Birds Aren't Real* Bird Drone Field Guide.

PIGEON DRONE

Have you ever seen a baby pigeon? You haven't, have you? No one has, not in many, many years. They used to be everywhere. You couldn't walk out of your front door in New York City in the 1930s without those little guys scurrying around everywhere. Today, there are millions of grown-up pigeons in New York, but not a *baby* pigeon to be seen anywhere. That's because they come out of the factory as adults. This is one of the many smoking guns (emitting chimney levels of smoke—*chimney* levels) of the bird drone surveillance crisis.

As you may have guessed, the pigeon drone is used primarily for urban surveillance. It specializes in up-close monitoring. Unlike most other bird drones, it's designed to get very close to human beings—sometimes close enough to touch. However, most people aren't willing to *actually* touch the pigeon drones because they're "dirty." This is by design; it allows the pigeon drone to observe its target from a close proximity without being swatted away. They are the perfect "boots on the ground" surveillance tool for the government, and the worst thing to happen in the history of New York City, or any city on earth for that matter. They are also prolific defecators, and as we'll learn in the Frequently Asked Questions of the book, bird poop is a powerful tracking device. Unless you decide to devote your entire life to spreading the word about bird surveillance in a dense urban environment (which is a very commendable life path) we recommend living off the grid where you can be far away from the dirty swarms of these feathered demons.

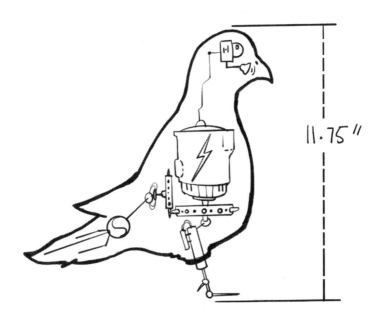

SEAGULL DRONE

The seagull drone is designed for two purposes. The first is aquatic surveillance. The federal government likes to know what is happening on land *and* on sea. A lot of shady business is discussed aboard boats, far away from the nearest American shore. International waters are a great place to plan a coup d'état (trust me), but a seagull drone is always close by, listening carefully to your plans.

The more egregious crime is the seagull's secondary purpose: DNA harvesting.

Has a seagull ever swooped down and stolen your food on the beach? Do you wonder why they do that? Seagulls are supposed to have their own food, provided by their mother—Mother Nature. So why would they need *our* food? It's actually quite simple. They are hunting for the DNA we leave behind through our saliva. After we take a bite of our lunch, seagulls will begin their assault, even going so far as to snatch food right out of our hands. These robots are not only thieves, they are rude. Once they've secured your saliva, they transmit the data immediately to the Pentagon, where it is stored for biodata harvesting. Also, "seagulls"? The "sea" part makes sense, but what is a "gull"? The existence of a seagull suggests that a "landgull" also exists. Where are these landgulls? Wherever they are, I hate them with all of the guts in my body.

BLUEBIRD DRONE

Known for its beauty and majestic colors, the bluebird is *extremely dangerous*. This drone is designed mainly for retina scanning. Its bright blue-and-orange coloring is meant to draw the admiring eyes of civilians. These admiring eyes are then scanned by the bluebird for biometric data and stored in a comprehensive government database.

Avoid bluebird drones as much as possible and never look directly at them, no matter how pretty they are. And trust me, they will be pretty. They are gorgeous. It's sort of like how you are not supposed to look at the sun, but the sun is, in theory, the prettiest possible thing you could look at. A ball of gorgeous life-giving light. I try to sneak some peeks at it sometimes. I looked at it for a few seconds too long last year and I couldn't see the color blue for a couple months, which made the whole bluebird-retina thing a lot easier to deal with.

There are many bird drone models that are similarly beautiful, such as the robin and the golden pheasant. Avoid looking at any of them! The more pretty a bird is, the more certain you can be that it's designed to scan your retinas.

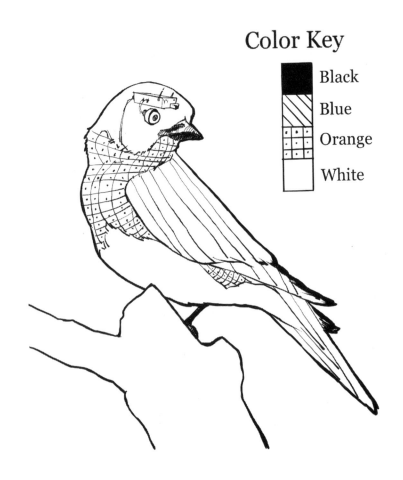

Color Key

Black

Blue

Orange

White

VULTURE DRONE

Vultures' responsibilities fall under the Public Sanitation Department. They are used to keep the highways and transit areas free of roadkill. Many people talk about Artificial Intelligence and automation threatening human workers in the future, but what they don't realize is that this has already been happening for 20 years. The Public Sanitation Department in the US has allocated $0 to roadkill cleanup since 2001. This is because the *second* a motor vehicle hits a real animal, vulture drones swoop in and scrape the roads clean, taking all those gross remains away with them to some unknown location in the sky, and all those jobs away from good, honest sanitation workers.

There are rumors that the vulture drones have been dropping off roadkill in the middle of the ocean for many years. If you look at satellite images from space, you can even see an island forming in the middle of the Atlantic, right where we suspect they've been dumping thousands of tons of roadkill for decades. Someday, I would love to go to Roadkill Island. I want to plant a Birds Aren't Real flag on it and declare it our sovereign nation. I hope to see you *all* there.

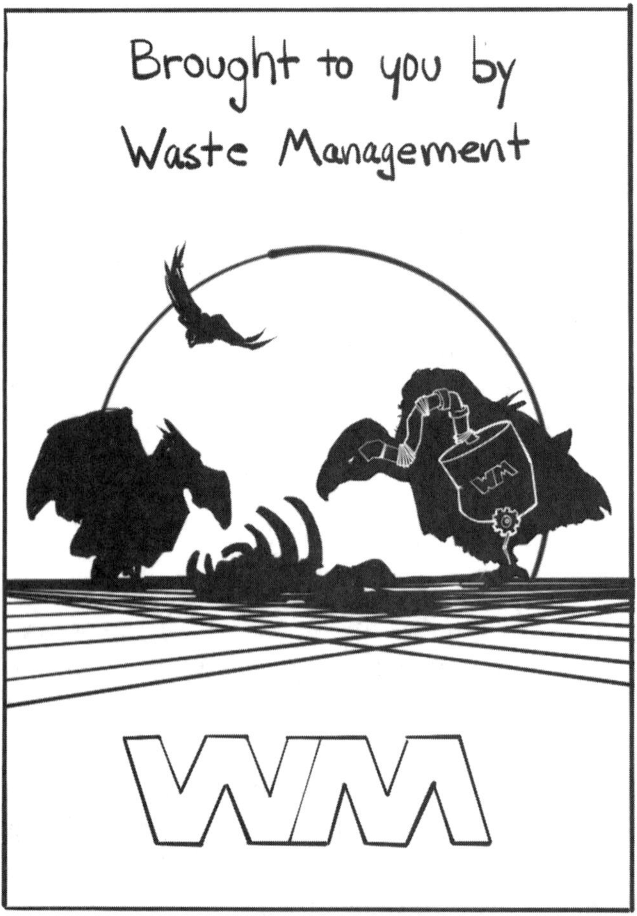
Brought to you by
Waste Management
WM
WM

GOOSE DRONE

The goose drone is specifically designed to serve as crowd control in parks and other recreational areas. A lot of loitering and "vagrant" activity takes place in these types of settings, so the government likes to monitor them closely. Allen Dulles, director of the CIA in the fifties, is on record as saying, "I hate the riffraff and the teen scum. We need to snuff out delinquent behavior in our parks. I'd prefer to just have every park in the United States paved over, but if we can't do that, then let's at least send some bird drones in to monitor them." When a goose drone detects illicit behavior, it charges the offender(s) and sends them running. If you have ever been chased by a goose at the park, that means you were deemed a "possible threat and/or nuisance."

Although their main domain is the parks, goose drones are occasionally used in more high-stakes missions. Because goose drones are relatively cheap to manufacture, they're great for "suicide missions," such as the now-famous attack on US Airways Flight 1549. On January 15th, 2009, a pilot named Sully Sullenberger was flying an Airbus A320 out of New York City when a flock of goose drones flew into the plane's engine. Sully narrowly avoided disaster by performing an emergency landing in the Hudson River, saving the lives of the 150 passengers on board. This event has been nicknamed the "Miracle on the Hudson," but the government refers to it as the "Failure Over Midtown," because the intent was to kill Sully Sullenberger—Sully was a prominent Bird Truther, and the government wanted to silence him. This detail was left out of the 2016 film *Sully*, starring the cowardly Tom Hanks.

OWL DRONE

Think you're safe from surveillance at night? Think again. The government knows all the best surveilling is done at night. That's where the owl drone excels. Owl drones are loaded with night-vision surveillance cameras and sonar so that they can keep spying on you long after the sun goes down.

Although their *primary* purpose is nighttime surveillance, there is an even stranger secondary purpose of the owl drone: they're a litmus test for what we, the public, are willing to believe. There are several things the public accepts as fact about owls that are just not logical or possible. For instance, owls have *gigantic* eyes and tiny little beaks. Look at any other "bird" of prey and tell me that that checks out. And why on earth are they so invested in learning how quickly our children can eat lollipops? There's no reasonable explanation for this—it's a total non sequitur.

Still not convinced? How about the fact that owls can spin their heads 360 degrees around in a circle. *Seriously?* If you are reading this, then that means you are a real organic being, I hope. Try spinning *your* head around all the way around like that. Can you do it? No! Because real living things would snap their neck bones. Let's be very clear: owls do not make sense at all, and that's intentional. They're designed to see how stupid we are, and it turns out we're *pretty* stupid. For the love of God, we cannot keep falling for this!

HAWK DRONE

Considered the "Alpha" model, the hawk is one of the most powerful bird drones in existence. It is used primarily for intimidation. Think of any villain in history: what do they have by their side? Henchmen. Thugs. Tough guys who carry crowbars and break kneecaps. The government is the villain in this situation, and their henchmen have claws and beaks and go by the name "hawks." They will do unspeakably horrible things. For instance, hawks have stolen 20 of my dogs. They just swoop down and carry them away. Every time I get a new dog, another hawk comes in and takes it away. I eventually stopped getting new dogs. So now, the hawks will fly down and rail into me while I'm walking alone in alleyways, slamming me against walls. They'll scrape their claws against the windows of my van when I'm sleeping at night, letting me know they're there. They'll rip my backpack off my back and push me into fountains. They are bullies, plain and simple.

If there are any hawks reading this: you do not scare me. I am like Captain America and no matter how many times you knock me down, I'll get back up. And one day I will metaphorically acquire superhero serum like Captain America did, and I will metaphorically beat you up by deactivating you. How about that? Who's the tough guy now?

HUMMINGBIRD DRONE

WARNING: EXTREMELY DANGEROUS. Hummingbirds are attack drones, and they are the evilest, most dangerous assassins in history. Silent and deadly as samurai, except tiny, and fluttery, and a bird.

Hummingbird drones are able to emit an untraceable and very deadly poison via their beaks. They'll poke into a target's neck like adorable little spears, release their poison, and then quickly flutter away, vanishing into thin air. These birds are very fast and very small. They're able to complete a "job" without attracting much attention. It's estimated that hummingbird drones have killed over 300 Bird Truthers to date. It's possible the number is way higher than that. Some scholars say it's more like *3,000.*

There are a few ways a Bird Truther can protect him or herself from this reality. A lot of us wear chain mail under our clothes at all times, so that the hummingbird's beak cannot pierce our skin. Some carry tennis rackets everywhere they go, so that they can swat hummingbird drones away before they get too close.

Unfortunately, these measures don't exactly cut it, because the hummingbird drone is designed with a backup weapon: a GUN! The hummingbird drone can shoot a .22 LR bullet from its beak with the same velocity and accuracy as a regular firearm, but it's twice as deadly because they *always fire from point-blank range.*

This is why we officially recommend that everyone in attendance at any Bird Truther meeting or rally carry a whistle. If you see a hummingbird in the vicinity, you can simply blow your whistle (or a similar noisemaking device) to warn everyone that there's an assassination attempt in progress. I have saved thousands of lives over the years by doing this. Unfortunately, I was born too late to save president, bird-truth martyr, and all-around great guy John F. Kennedy, which is one of the principal regrets of my life.

OSTRICH DRONE

Ostriches are essentially the construction workers of the government surveillance drone lineup. You'll learn more about this later, but the government has had hundreds of thousands of power lines erected across the country, which act as charging stations for bird drones. The country's *actual* electricity needs are served by underground wires. The government wanted to design a bird drone with an elongated neck capable of reaching down into the ground to repair and maintain our electrical grid. Much like vulture drones, this is a tragic example of robots stealing human jobs 20 years before anyone thought it would happen. There are rumors that ostriches only live in Africa, but this is classic media misdirection. I have seen ostriches here in the States hundreds of times, they just often have their heads underground and are easily mistaken for bushes and stuff.

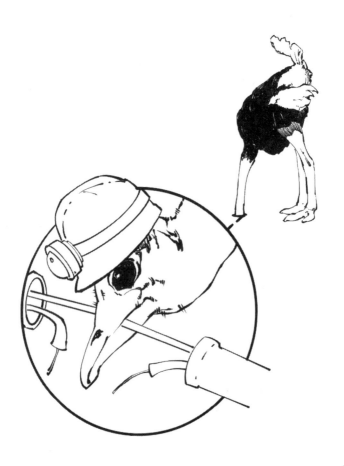

PARROT DRONE

The parrot drone is designed for linguistic analysis. It can record and process human speech. This helps the government improve the language-learning data models that they feed into bird drone software across the board.

Parrot drones are designed to play back recorded audio to government officials *only*. For instance, parrot drones will linger around a Bird Truther meeting and then fly over to the local senator's house to play back the meeting for them. The government messed up, though. Due to a few manufacturing errors, the parrots have a foundational glitch where they will repeat things they hear *all* the time to *anyone*. This became a huge problem when millions of parrots were released into the public from the factories. They started repeating bits of conversation right in front of the people they were recording. The CIA thought their plans were ruined, but they underestimated the stupidity of the American public. People just completely accepted that this sort of bird is able to talk. They didn't even question it! Even though no other bird or animal does *anything* like this. Even though the nature of a bird's beak is so different from that of the human mouth that it could never produce the same sounds. Unbelievable.

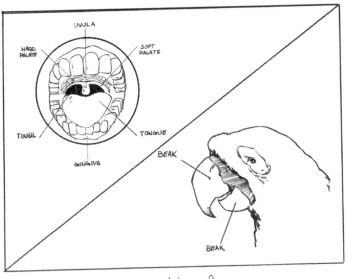

"These are capable of Making the Same sounds" – Sheeple

DODO

This bird went extinct long before the government started exterminating the real birds in the fifties. A bird untouched by the evil, metallic hands of Uncle Sam. A bird preserved in innocence and safety, killed off by natural causes like good ol' fashioned bullets, not by poisonous toxins sprayed from B-52B bombers. We love the dodo for what it represents. A precious creature existing as it should. I hope that one day we find dodo DNA like in the movie *Jurassic Park* and we can bring them back. That would be so cool. This is the bird-filled future that we are fighting for, brothers and sisters.

4

FREQUENTLY ASKED QUESTIONS

You probably still have a lot of lingering questions. Ones that may be preventing you from keeping an open mind about bird surveillance. You may be thinking to yourself, "Birds must be real! There is evidence of them all around me!"

No they're not, and no there isn't.

The government, to its credit, did a good job covering their tracks. They thought of everything, taking careful steps to make it seem like birds are still living, breathing creatures. You must not be fooled by their tricks. So, I've decided to dedicate a section of this book to answering any remaining questions you may have. This section will cover in depth the many ways in which the government has tried to cover up what they've done. I will also address some questions about the Birds Aren't Real movement in general. These are all questions that I have been asked hundreds of times over the years.

Hopefully this section will clear things up so that you can maintain an open mind going forward on the path toward enlightenment.

Q. WHAT IS THIS MOVEMENT'S PURPOSE?

To spread awareness, first and foremost. Sadly, 99.99% of the American population still believes that birds are real. They're living in a bubble of ignorance, going about their lives as if everything is normal. As if everything is "okay." They're allowing themselves to be manipulated, spied on, and made fools of. We need to wake them from this trance, otherwise we'll never be able to fight back. You can't fight if you're asleep.

The Birds Aren't Real movement originally formed back in the 1970s, when the government was still in the early stages of killing off the bird population. Those original Birds Aren't Real activists were trying to *prevent* bird surveillance before it went too far. They hoped that if they rallied the people of this great nation against the tyrannical shadow government, then the government could be forced to discontinue its bird surveillance project. The activists wanted to achieve this *before* the bird population was completely killed off.

Unfortunately, the cries of these early Bird Truthers fell on deaf ears. The government continued its bird surveillance program for decades (it continues to this day). By now, the entire bird population is long dead. It is too late for prevention. But it might not be too late to undo what's been done. There are still billions of *real* birds living in other countries. With a little effort, we could reintroduce real birds back into America and let them begin repopulating. Perhaps someday, the bird population can be totally restored to pre-1970s levels (see pg. 176 for more on repopulation).

But we will never achieve that beautiful goal without spreading AWARENESS. We need to teach every man, woman, and child in this country the truth about bird surveillance. We cannot undo the horrors of bird surveillance without a massive awareness campaign, followed by a massive revolt. Our hope is that if the movement grows large enough, then the government will not be able to ignore us. There needs to be more of *us* than there are of *them*. Only then can we start making demands.

What we would like to achieve is full repopulation by 2030. We also demand that the bird drones be deactivated immediately, and that legislation be passed to ban all use of bird-based surveillance in the future.

I personally hope that this book you're reading right now is the spark that lights the fire.

I want you to picture something: right now, the entire country is living in a dark cave. The secret truths of the world are written on the walls of that cave. Technically speaking, the truth is right there in front of everyone's eyes, but they can't actually see it because it's too dark in the cave. If only there was one little spark to light a fire, then the cave would become illuminated enough to read what is written on the walls. I'd like this book to be that spark. The spark that lights the way. The spark that leads you out of the darkness. The spark that reveals the secret truths written on the walls, mere inches in front of you. (This is just a metaphor, to be clear. Do not light this book on fire.)

Q. WHAT ABOUT BIRD EGGS?

When the government began developing bird drone prototypes, they knew they had to make them look as realistic as possible so that they wouldn't arouse suspicion. They couldn't just release a bunch of tinpot flying machines into the air that beep and boop and have wires hanging from them. They needed to look like real birds, but also *function* like real birds. That meant they needed to have the same bodily functions as living, breathing birds— including laying eggs.

Inside every bird drone there is a small compartment that houses a few "eggs." These eggs are created synthetically in a laboratory. They are *not* organic things formed by the miracle of nature. The bird drones are designed to randomly "lay" these eggs, but they are not actually giving "birth" in any sense whatsoever. They are simply ejecting the synthetically created eggs from their robot bodies. This whole process of bird drones laying eggs is all for show. Once again, it's all about making the bird drones seem like living creatures.

You may be saying to yourself, "Wait a second. That can't be. I eat eggs every morning." I'm sorry to say, but no, you don't. The goopy yellow-and-white substance you see when you crack open a bird "egg" is 100% lab-cultured protein. It is perfectly edible, but it's not actual yolk. The government knew that when they killed off the bird population, they needed to find some way to keep the poultry industry going. It would be suspicious if there were suddenly no eggs at the grocery stores. That's why they put an incredible amount of time, effort, and money into developing synthetic eggs—ones that can be eaten just like an organic egg. That carton of eggs you buy every week is actually just a big carton of CIA science.

If this sounds outlandish, I encourage you to do some research on your own. Look into "animal-free eggs" online and see what you find. This information is freely available.

There is something even *more* sinister going on with eggs, though. This goes beyond simple deception. A few years ago, a small group of Birds Aren't Real activists managed to breach a CIA server and leak some highly classified research documents that tell us a lot about the shadow government's egg operation. The CIA scientists who created synthetic poultry have *also* been studying the science of "biotracking."

WHAT IS BIOTRACKING?

"Biotracking" is the science of predicting human behavior through the study of biological chemistry. For example, if a human being is low on vitamin D, you might infer that they don't get a lot of sunlight. That might lead you to infer that they don't go outside much. That might lead you to infer that they have antisocial tendencies. *That* might lead you to infer that they have the potential to be violent, rebellious, or generally transgressive. You can see why the government might be interested in this science. There is a lot you can learn from each person's unique biochemistry. The more you learn, the better predictions you (or the government) can make.

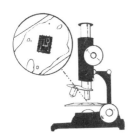

Government scientists are actively working on developing an atom-sized chip that, if swallowed by a human, could evaluate their biochemistry and send that information back to the government to be analyzed. They are trying to perfect this technology by the end of 2024. Once they mass-produce these biotracking chips, they intend to plant them in eggs. They are using eggs for this because the vast majority of Americans eat eggs in some form or another.

Producing these specialized biotracking eggs costs an enormous amount of money, and there are sometimes shortages of the required materials. Supply chain issues often slow production to a crawl. This is the reason for the rising cost of eggs in recent years.

Q. WHAT IS BIRD POOP?

Every bird drone is designed to expel a small amount of oily, synthetic liquid (that resembles poop) every few hours. Much like bird drones laying fake eggs, this is all just for "show." The bird drones do not actually eat,

Bird Poop = Tracking Device

digest, or expel organic matter. What you think of as "bird shit" is in fact *bull*shit.

But, once again, there is something more sinister going on. This synthetic liquid expelled by the bird drones is also used to track human targets.

You're probably familiar with the idea of a tracking device—the kind of device that cops in TV shows and movies put on the bad guy's car to track them. Or maybe you're familiar with how wildlife scientists put tracking collars on endangered animals to monitor their patterns. But GPS technology is *far* more advanced than you realize. Leaked research documents show that the United States government has developed a GPS tracking chip that is roughly the size of a grain of sand. Despite being so small, these tracking chips are just as powerful as the GPS technology in your car or smartphone.

Bird drones are able to expel a load of "poop" that has one of these tracking chips mixed in at will. Whenever you see bird poop splattered on someone's car (maybe even your own), it's likely that person has been marked as a person of interest. They are being closely tracked by the government, for whatever reason. We in the Birds Aren't Real community suggest that you routinely check your car and even your body for bird poop. If you find any, wash it off *immediately*.

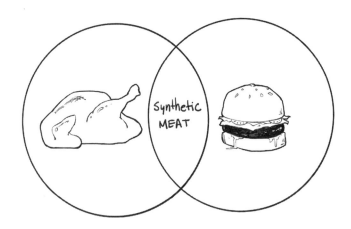

Q. WHAT IS BIRD MEAT?

This is the most common question I get from Birds Aren't Real skeptics. People are constantly telling me, "Peter, birds *must* be real, because I eat them all the time."

No, you don't. The bird meat you've been consuming all your life, whether you buy it at the grocery store or order it at a restaurant, is not meat at all. Modern-day poultry is comprised of meat alternatives such as pea protein, chickpea, soy, tempeh, etc. It has been carefully prepared to look and taste like real meat, but it is not. Even that Thanksgiving turkey you eat every year is completely vegetarian.

But wait, what about roadkill? I get that question a lot, too. You've probably seen dead birds on the side of the highway plenty of times, with their guts and innards splattered all over the pavement. Certainly, those *have* to be real birds, right? Wrong. Those are indeed robotic bird drones. If that sounds outlandish to you, it's because you have the wrong idea of what a "robot" is. Before we continue, let's talk about what the word "robot" means in the modern era.

WHAT WE MEAN WHEN WE TALK ABOUT "ROBOTS"

When you hear the word "robot," you probably picture some clanky metallic thing full of wires, chips, bolts, and blinking lights. This classic image of the "robot" is way outdated. It's important to know that the government has developed technology far beyond your wildest imagination. This technology is kept secret for various reasons. If you were to see it, you would hardly be able to process it. It would be like a caveman seeing a modern-day smartphone.

Except you have seen it. The bird drones are an example of the government's superior technology. They are robots in the sense that they are manmade and not sentient, but the way they are designed and constructed defies all expectations of what a robot is.

Bird drones are built out of an ultra-lightweight metallic alloy. This material is very thin and extremely malleable, much like a living creature's skin. The wires and chips you associate with robots *are* inside the bird drones, but they are carefully disguised as organic materials. The bird drone's central control system (or "brain") is a very small chip, which is encased inside a fleshy ball of synthetic material that resembles a living creature's brain. The various wires running throughout the bird drones are microscopically thin and run through fleshy tubes that resemble veins. Small cameras are concealed within rubbery orbs that act as the creature's "eyes." Every component of a bird drone is meticulously designed to look like an organic body part.

Even if you were to carefully dissect a bird drone, you would have trouble telling it apart from an actual bird. The bird drones even have artificial hearts, which have no actual function—they are just there to throw you off in case you decide to take a closer look at the innards of a bird drone. Despite my hatred of bird drones and what they represent, there is no denying that they are marvels of modern engineering.

Q. WHAT ABOUT MIGRATION?

Ah, migration. It is one of the strangest phenomena in the animal kingdom. Why *do* birds fly south for the winter, anyway? Science will tell you it's to look for alternate food sources, or to stay warm until the winter weather passes. THESE ARE LIES. There is no actual historical account of birds migrating. Animals don't go on vacation! Migration is a **fake** phenomenon that did not exist before the 1970s. The whole notion of "migration" was invented by the government. Birds do not migrate, but bird *drones* do.

Why? To traffic drugs.

A BRIEF HISTORY OF GOVERNMENT INVOLVEMENT IN THE DRUG TRADE

In 1979, a group of socialist revolutionaries called the Sandinistas took power in Nicaragua. The United States government was concerned that the Sandinistas' socialist agenda would spread. So, they began sending money to a right-wing rebel group called the Contras, who were attempting to take back Nicaragua from the Sandinistas. This was done under the direction of President Ronald Reagan.

When Congress decided to stop allocating money toward funding the Contras, Reagan was unwilling to let the battle over Nicaragua end. So, he conspired with the CIA to find new ways to make money for the Contras. One of those ways was drug trafficking. The Contras had plentiful access to cocaine in Nicaragua. The CIA helped them set up a massive cocaine trafficking ring so they could use the profits in their war against the Sandinistas. The American shadow government willingly looked the other way as these Contra rebels trafficked cocaine into various countries—including the United States. Many people believe the crack epidemic of the 1980s was a direct result of this.

> Drug trafficking turned out to be a great way for the shadow government to make money "off the books." To this day, the American government continues to fund drug trafficking operations. They take a cut of the profits and use it to fund their sinister and illegal operations.

The American government likes to keep a steady supply of narcotics coming into the country. Aside from profiting off drug trafficking operations, they also benefit from the effects these drugs have on the people. Drugs keep the population distracted and complacent. Bird drones are frequently used to retrieve drugs from countries like Colombia, Bolivia, and Mexico. This is the **real** reason birds fly south.

Organizations that keep a close eye on the border (such as the Drug Enforcement Agency and Immigration and Customs Enforcement) don't know about this bird drone drug-fetching operation. Looping in agencies like ICE and the DEA would only create a bigger risk of leaks. The decision-makers at the highest levels of government like to keep the "underlings" in the dark about what's *really* going on. This is called *compartmentalization*. There is a chain-of-command in the government, and at every link in the chain, people only know what they *need* to know. That's why border patrol agents in the United States are blissfully unaware that "birds" are trafficking drugs into the country just above their heads.

Sometimes, birds that are *not* programmed to cross the border do so anyway because they glitch out and become confused. The government tries to minimize this as much as possible. Every drone is very expensive to make and maintain, so they don't want to lose any. That's why all the bird drones that are not meant to leave the country are designed with an internal kill switch that is activated if they cross the border. This automatic kill switch causes the bird drone to power down and fall to the ground, at which point a government operative can swoop in to retrieve it and bring it back to headquarters to be debugged.

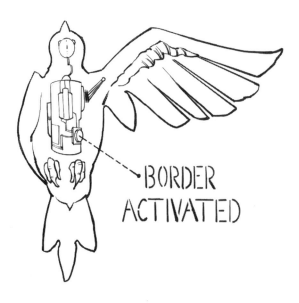

BORDER ACTIVATED

Q. BUT DO REAL BIRDS EVER FLY INTO THE US FROM OTHER COUNTRIES?

Yes, occasionally real birds will fly in from countries such as Canada and Mexico, and the American government is **not** happy about it. They don't want real birds cluttering the skies and getting in the way of the bird drones. Also, real birds tend to have a volatile reaction to the bird drones. We believe that the drones trigger an "uncanny valley" feeling in real birds. The sight of bird drones makes them feel scared, angry, or both. They will begin to squawk at the drones and sometimes even attempt to attack them. So, the government tries to keep real birds out of the country as much as possible. **Our country's entire border is equipped with technology that emits a high-frequency, ultrasonic sound to frighten off birds.**

Q. HOW ARE BIRD DRONES POWERED?

The earliest bird drone prototypes were battery-powered, but the government realized that that would be a logistical nightmare. They would have to constantly monitor the power levels of each bird drone, recall them when they were close to running out of juice, recharge them, and then rerelease them. It was highly inefficient, so they quickly developed a better solution: power lines. Modern-day bird drones can quickly recharge by perching atop power lines for a few minutes. It is the same process that happens when you charge a phone by placing it on a wireless charging pad. This is the reason you see birds perching on power lines so often.

It's also the reason that you see power lines *at all*. Come on, you think that in the year 2024 we still need to be using big, long, airborne wires to make everything run? All the real power is either wireless or underground (and serviced by ostrich drones, as we learned in the field guide).

Theoretically, if there were no more power lines, the bird drones would run out of juice and die forever. Unfortunately, damaging power lines is highly illegal . . . But it's also very *easy*. See pg. 171 if you're interested in learning more.

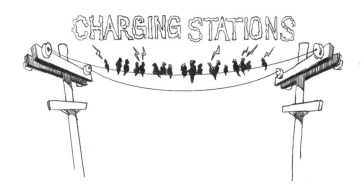

Q. DO YOU HATE BIRDS?

No! This is a very ugly misconception that people have about the Birds Aren't Real movement. We do not hate birds—we hate bird *drones*.

Most of us Birds Aren't Real activists are very passionate about animal rights. We love animals, birds included. In fact, nothing makes us sadder than the fact that we may never see a *real* bird ever again, because they have all been poisoned to death by the US government. We may never get to marvel at the majestic beauty of a Bohemian waxwing (*Bombycilla garrulus*) as it gently munches some berries on a warm summer day. We may never get to enjoy the gorgeous song of the common nightingale (*Luscinia megarhynchos*). We may never get to experience the simple joy of feeding a gorgeous wood duck (*Aix sponsa*) down by the local pond. Instead, we have to endure the cold, cruel gaze of the *fake* birds that are all around us. Nothing is more depressing than that. It's like living in a world that's been drained of all its beauty.

We don't hate birds. We hate what's been *done* to them. We hate what they've been replaced by. That is why we're advocating for repopulation. We are not just demanding that the government deactivate the bird drones. We are demanding that they help reintroduce *real* birds back into the American ecosystem. We are not fighting this battle out of hatred. We are fighting it out of love. I would love to live in a world where birds are plentiful and thriving. I would love to leave my house some morning and see a sparrow perched atop my mailbox, a canary perched atop a nearby tree, a robin perched atop my roof. That thought almost brings a tear to my eye. But for now, all we have are cold replicas of the real thing, spying on us on behalf of the government. Let us take a brief moment of silence for all the dead birds before we continue.

Please pause here for a 30-second moment of silence.

Q. IF THIS IS ALL REAL, HOW HAVE I NOT HEARD ABOUT IT UNTIL NOW?

The Birds Aren't Real movement has been aggressively silenced by the government from the very beginning. We have repeatedly been blackmailed, censored, shadowbanned, and in some cases *disappeared*. The reason you haven't heard about any of this is because very powerful forces have gone to great lengths to hide it from you.

Q. WHAT IF I HAVE A PET BIRD IN MY HOME?

First of all, remain calm. You *are* in danger, but stay calm. If you have a pet bird in your home, that means the government has been monitoring you around the clock. Their propaganda machine probably convinced you to purchase a pet bird in the first place. By now, they likely know everything about you. That includes your habits, your schedule, and even the layout of your home. Worst of all, they know that you're reading this book. That means you are most likely a person of interest—that is not good.

My advice would be to calmly pack your things in the middle of the night and leave. Make sure your bird does not see you leave. Exit through a back door, or even via the roof if you have to. Once you're out of there, don't return to your home under any circumstances, even if you forgot something important, like your shoes or your insulin.

Unfortunately, you're just going to have to find a new place to live. Try to keep a low profile while you search for your new home. Stay vigilant and make sure no birds are monitoring you. Once you've found a new place to stay—and I hope this goes without saying—DO NOT GET ANOTHER PET BIRD!

I understand this may be difficult. Even though you are now realizing your beloved pet bird was a surveillance drone the whole time, you may still have feelings for it. Just try to remind yourself that it is not a living, breathing creature, and it does not love you.

5

THE REAL HISTORY OF AMERICA

When I first learned about bird surveillance, I couldn't believe I'd been told such a huge lie all my life. I started to wonder to myself, what other lies have I been told? Is *everything* I've been taught a lie? It turns out, yes, it is, and the same goes for you.

If you've received a public-school education in America, you probably *think* you have a pretty good understanding of American history. Unfortunately, you don't—not even close. The American government has full control over what is taught in schools. They design the curriculums, and they don't care about teaching you the *true* story of America. What they teach you is a mostly fictional account of our nation's history. That's why I've spent the last few years of my life reeducating myself using sources that are untainted by the government. That's hard to do, because books, websites, and other sources are heavily monitored by the shadow government. Any *true* information that they don't want you to know is quickly censored. It's only in the deepest recesses of the dark web that you can find real information.

After years of doing my own research, I now have a very good understanding of the true story of America. Once again, almost none of this information has been taught to you in school because the powers-that-be don't want you to know this stuff. They want you brainwashed, walking through life in a zombified state, with a storybook understanding of American history. Well, it's time to throw the storybook away and dive into the real stuff. What follows is a brief overview of American history.

My hope is that someday, the American school system gets reformed and they start teaching this material. I have traveled to dozens of different school districts throughout the US and spoken to principals and superintendents about implementing this curriculum, but so far none of them have had the courage to do it.

Your reeducation begins now. Study this information very carefully, and never let anyone tell you that it isn't true.

THE GREAT REBELLION

In 1607 a gang of British adventurers left Great Britain and sailed to North America. They were sick of the stuffy old Queen and all her rules, and wanted to get as far from Great Britain as possible. They found life in North America to be pretty nice. The land was good for farming, there were mild climates, and the native people seemed friendly. Word spread about this cool new continent and other British people who were also sick of the Queen and her rules started coming over. After years of living in colonies in North America, these settlers started to not really "feel" British at all anymore, so they got upset when the British Crown tried to tax them. It was like the Queen was reaching across the entire ocean, sticking her hand in their pockets, and taking a cut of what little money they had. Something had to be done about this.

THE THIRTEEN COLONIES

Soon the Thirteen Colonies were formed (originally the "Fourteen Colonies" until they kicked out New Jersey), led by the amazing George Washington. The Colonies wanted to form an independent nation, and they were willing to fight the British Crown for it if they had to. This fight for freedom from the tyrannical British Crown is called the American Revolution. The apex of the American Revolution was in 1812, when George Washington led his colonial army across the Delaware Ocean and stormed the gates of Gettysburg, a city that was occupied by the British at the time. Washington and his rebels knocked the absolute hell out of the British and declared their independence from Great Britain. They vowed to never let a British guy tell them what to do ever again. This was the beginning of the United States of America.

THE BUILDING OF AN EMPIRE

Washington and his gang of newly independent Americans got to work on building the greatest empire in the history of civilization. For a while American territory only extended to the Mississippi River. Everything west of that belonged to the French. We soon discovered the French were easy to push around, so we made them sell us this land at a crazy discount. Americans continued to push farther and farther west, led by a brave explorer named Lewison Clark. Lewison pushed all the way to the Pacific Coast. America had quickly grown into a sprawling empire, reaching from the Atlantic to the Pacific. Unfortunately, it took a lot of slave labor to build America into the mighty empire that it was, and some Americans began to question the ethics of slavery. One of those men was a gangly old chap by the name of Abraham Lincoln, our 16th president. A brutal, bloody Civil War was fought over slavery that pitted "brother against brother." The Civil War threatened to rip America in two. The government learned a harsh lesson from this: the common people were willing to fight to the death for their beliefs. That was a scary idea for the government.

After the Civil War came Reconstruction. America was trying to repair the damage done by the Civil War. People were still really mad about what went down, especially the guys that lost. It was an all-around pretty bad era in America. Around this time, the American government began to think they needed to keep a very close eye on the people. They were worried we would use our freedom to rebel against them, the same way our forefathers did against the British Crown. Simply put, the government needed a way to spy on us to make sure we weren't getting too unruly. Remember, this was still a relatively primitive time in history. There were no recording devices. Things weren't the way they are today, when the government can just tap your phone or send an owl to sit outside your house. The only way they could spy on people back then was "clandestine human intelligence."

Clandestine Human Intelligence: The gathering of information using undercover human sources (i.e., spies)

OPERATION WALLFLOWER

Around 1870, Ulysses S. Grant instituted a top-secret program called "Operation Wallflower." His cabinet created a list of hundreds of "people of interest." These were Americans that the Grant administration deemed

"subversives." In other words, they were people who were likely to rebel against the government. Operation Wallflower was an attempt to "bug" the homes of these subversive citizens. A series of very small men were hired to infiltrate their homes, hide in their walls, listen to everything they were saying, and report back to the government. Grant jokingly gave these tiny men the ironic nickname "Big Brothers." (Many people think George Orwell coined the phrase "Big Brother" in his novel *1984,* but the phrase predates that book by 70 years.)

The little men were forced to endure harsh conditions, hiding in people's walls for up to 72 hours at a time. At this time, labor unions were a new phenomenon in the United States. Unions were having success improving working conditions in various industries. So, the Big Brothers attempted to form a union of their own called "The Spiers Union." They demanded more breaks, higher pay, and benefits. The federal government was infuriated by their attempt to unionize and decided to shut down Operation Wallflower in 1872. The little men were fired and forced to find new lines of work.

THE INDUSTRIAL REVOLUTION AND ITS CONSEQUENCES

The Industrial Revolution was a period in America when new technology was being developed at a rapid pace. Innovative tools, machines, and other technologies were invented to make manufacturing—and life in general— quicker and easier. Things like the steam engine, the sewing machine, and the automobile were results of the Industrial Revolution, but there were much more sinister motivations behind it.

Beginning in the late 18th century, the American government was trying to develop sophisticated spy technology. Analog surveillance (i.e., little men hiding in walls) was not cutting it. So, they began giving out generous grants to inventors and scientists so that they could develop innovative new methods of spying. Basically all of the smartest people alive between 1750 and 1910 were funded by the American government, including geniuses like Thomas Edison, Albert Einstein, Alexander Graham Bell, Nikola Tesla, and countless others.

Some of the brilliant minds who received money from the government to develop spy technology decided to invent completely different things instead. Albert Einstein, for example, received a grant of $30,000 to develop a "high-powered listening device," and when he told the American government two years later that he had finally made "a world-changing breakthrough," it turned out that he had only discovered the theory of relativity. The American government was so furious with him that they tried to have him extradited from Germany and thrown in an American prison. However, some of these government-funded scientists *did* come through, developing cutting-edge devices that laid the groundwork for mass surveillance.

EARLY SURVEILLANCE TECHNOLOGY

The phonograph

Thomas Edison's phonograph was a primitive device that could record and play back audio. It was an important jumping-off point for the invention of the microphone. And guess what's in *every single bird drone*? That's right, a microphone. That wouldn't be possible without the phonograph setting the blueprint. The original phonograph was big, clunky, and didn't have very good sound quality, but President Rutherford B. Hayes said of the invention, "I hope one day someone invents a phonograph so small that we can hide one in the home of every single American citizen." He really said that.

The kinetoscope

The kinetoscope was the precursor to the film camera. People would peer through a peephole and see a rapid-fire series of images that looked like filmed footage. Although the original kinetoscope of 1891 was very primitive and mostly used to view softcore pornography, it set the groundwork needed to develop the film camera years later. And do you know what the eyes of every bird drone are? **Cameras.** Thanks a lot, Thomas Edison, for inventing a porno machine that later became a dystopian surveillance tool. You are 100% implicated in the nightmare that we're experiencing today. I hate you so much.

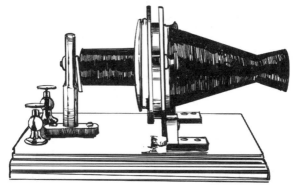

The telephone

You probably know that a guy named Alexander Graham Bell invented the telephone, but do you know *why*? It wasn't to make your life easier, that's for sure. Bell (colluding with the American government) wanted people to *think* the conversations they had on the phone with their friends, family, and co-conspirators were private. This is obviously not true. The original telephone was designed to be easily "bugged" by the government. A lot of people think bugging phones is a relatively new thing, but it's actually been done since 1876.

Although the Industrial Revolution happened entirely because the government was trying to bankroll the development of surveillance technology, some good things still came out of this era. New jobs were being created and the average American was having an okay time. The good times peaked in the 1920s, also known as the "Roaring Twenties." But unfortunately for everyone, the stock market crashed in 1929, and the Roaring Twenties quickly turned into the "Throw Yourself Off a Building Thirties." The economy collapsed almost completely, and the country experienced years of hardship. This was called the Great Depression, and it really *was* depressing. At the peak, as much as 24% of the population was unemployed. People were losing their jobs, living on the street, and going hungry. The government feared that all this hardship and unrest would cause Americans to revolt. President Herbert Hoover was reported to have said, "One of these days all those bums on the street are going to get sick of eating garbage and they're gonna storm the White House. We need to step up our surveillance measures and make sure they don't get unruly."

But soon, there were bigger things to worry about. A really bad guy named Adolf Hitler was causing a lot of trouble in Germany. The Soviet Union seemed to be doing pretty well and a lot of people in the world were wondering if there might be something to this "communism" thing after all. This brings us to the 1940s, the Red Scare, and the early stages of bird surveillance. You were briefed on this in a previous chapter (see pg. 3). By now you know there was only *one* person who tried to stop bird surveillance: John F. Kennedy. To this day, he remains the only US president to ever try and do something about the bird drone program. In fact, America has had very few "good" presidents in its history. You've probably been taught they were "great men" or whatever, but they were mostly corrupt cowards who had absolutely no idea what they were doing. So, I'd like to end our history lesson by running through each American president and giving you a 100% accurate biography for all of them.

THE HALL OF PRESIDENTS

GEORGE WASHINGTON

The first President of the United States has often been compared to Jesus Christ in terms of wisdom and stature. Leading his band of rebels known as Patriots out from under Her Royal Majesty's wrinkled thumb, he founded the Thirteen Colonies and established a new form of government known as the United States of America. Under his leadership, the country flourished, but unfortunately he declined the offer to be made King of America.

JOHN ADAMS

Serving as the vice president under George Washington, John Adams quickly found himself the second President of the United States. He was a remarkable philosopher who enjoyed long walks by the swamp and playing with his two dogs, George and Washington. While John Adams did some great things, George Washington is still the best president ever and John knew this.

THOMAS JEFFERSON

The primary author of the Declaration of Independence, Thomas (known by his friends as Tommy Jeffs) found himself as the third President of the United States from 1801 to 1809. At the time he was the most physically attractive president the United States had ever seen (besides George Washington) and sought to build a nation where everyone was free from tyranny. He was also in the Broadway play *Hamilton* and has a beautiful singing voice.

JAMES MADISON

James (Jimmy) Madison was known as the "Father of the Constitution," much to Thomas Jefferson's dismay. This error in public perception was instigated by his writing of the Federalist Papers, which heavily criticized Tommy Jefferson's views and caused conflict between him and many members of the government. He was often seen at George Washington's grave, pleading for Washington's spirit to descend upon the nation and "save him from this torment." He was the commander in chief for the War of 1812, which was exactly 100 years before the *Titanic* sank into the Atlantic Ocean. Coincidence?

JAMES MONROE

James Monroe was not known for his good looks, but he was known for being the fifth President of the United States. He's considered the last of the original Founding Fathers, and he dedicated his presidency to "touring America and enjoying the luxuries that this rich land possesses." This did not go over well with the public, and he was often seen crying in the West Wing of the White House.

JOHN QUINCY ADAMS

Johnny "Nepotism" Adams, as his friends called him, was the sixth President of the United States and a staunch supporter of never embarrassing himself. He believed that all people should walk with dignity and do nothing to tarnish their reputations or bring humiliation upon themselves. Sadly, he collapsed on the floor of the House surrounded by every single person he knew, had a stroke, and died. We will never forget him. Not a great president (he was no George Washington) but he didn't do anything super bad. He was an okay president.

ANDREW JACKSON

Andrew Jackson was the seventh President of the United States and a hater of Native Americans. He will be remembered as a decently attractive guy with a great disdain for those who lived in America for thousands of years. He was definitely no George Washington, and was often overheard ranting about "that old bag the Queen," saying that "if she ever comes across the pond I'm gonna punch her up real good." He was a bad president.

MARTIN VAN BUREN

"Old Marty," as he was called by his mistress, was the eighth President of the United States and a lover of magic tricks. He would carry around a deck of cards and challenge his opponents to a barrage of devious card tricks, but his greatest trick of all was convincing America that a man who looked like he did should be allowed to be seen in public. He was one ugly guy.

WILLIAM HENRY HARRISON
The ninth President of the United States, William Henry Harrison served the shortest term in American history at only 32 measly days. He died of a cold right after being elected. This made him one of America's greatest presidents—he's definitely in the top five.

JOHN TYLER
"The man with two first names," as he was called by his mother, was our 10th President of the United States and William Henry Harrison's vice president. After getting over the cold that he spread to his predecessor, he led the country for a few years and, in the 1860s, founded the Confederacy, blaspheming the great nation that George Washington worked so hard to create.

JAMES K. POLK
"Old Polky," as he was called, was our 11th president and the last of the "strong presidents" to sit in office before the Civil War. He was responsible for buying many states and adding them to the laundry list of acquired land that the United States government sought to collect. He was a decently attractive man with broad shoulders and narrow hips. He accomplished a lot during his time in office and did not let Great Britain reclaim America, not that they tried.

ZACHARY TAYLOR

Our 12th, and by far the most physically unattractive, president to serve, Zachary Taylor sat in the White House for a little over a year before passing away. He owned 100 slaves, and was also a terrible supporter of the principles that George Washington tried to instill in his nation.

MILLARD FILLMORE

Old man Millard was a pale old duck with a love of mashed potatoes and sitting on his front porch whittling voodoo dolls of birds out of balsa wood. He loved to stab the voodoo dolls, which in his mind was like stabbing real birds, which he could not do due to his inability to climb trees and capture them. This is the first recorded president to hate birds.

FRANKLIN PIERCE

The 14th president would watch Millard Fillmore stab his voodoo doll birds with jealous rage, because he wanted to stab birds too. He spent much of his private life hunting for the rarest types of birds in the deep forests of America. He should've had his head examined, but sadly, medicine at the time was sorely lacking.

JAMES BUCHANAN

If being single makes you a great president, then James Buchanan was the best president in history (besides George Washington). "Old four-eyes Jimmy," as he was called, did not, in fact, have four eyes. He had two, and they never saw a woman in his bedroom. What was the outcome of our President never finding love? The Civil War started.

ABRAHAM LINCOLN

If you need the *Birds Aren't Real* book to tell you who Abraham Lincoln was, you might be a communist. "Honest Abe" was the most truthful president who ever lived. He never told a lie. His beard wasn't the best look for him, but he did pull it off at the time. Nowadays, his beard would not be considered "a good look." Thankfully, having scraggly facial hair does not prevent you from doing a bang-up job as president. Sadly, he was assassinated by John Wilkes Booth during a movie.

ANDREW JOHNSON

Our 17th president had the unfortunate task of avenging the assassination of Abraham Lincoln. He gathered a posse of government officials and stormed the gates of John Wilkes Booth's house, slaying him with his jewel-studded sword. He had a very American-sounding name. "Andrew Johnson." Has a nice ring to it. You know what doesn't have a nice ring to it? Bird drone surveillance.

ULYSSES S. GRANT

Ulysses has three s's in his name, but that didn't stop him from beating the bejesus out of the Confederates in the Civil War. As the general of the Union army, he was the one driving the tanks into Gettysburg and finally wiping that smug smile off Bobby E. Lee's stupid face.

What gives Bob the right to rebel in the first place? Who does he think he is? Well, he lost, Ulysses won, and that's all there is to it. He was rewarded for his bravery by being elected the 18th President of the United States, and began Reconstruction.

RUTHERFORD B. HAYES

If you search "1800s man" on Google, you'll probably get someone who looks like Rutherford B. Hayes. This didn't stop him from going to Harvard Law School, where he learned the art of persuasion, which came in handy when he was made the 19th president at a time of great unrest. His name "Rutherford" was a bold choice by his parents, but he really grew into it. He definitely *looks* like a Rutherford. He was an okay president.

JAMES GARFIELD

James Garfield was lazy, fat, and cynical. He also hated Mondays and was often spotted perched high atop a rock wall, trying to convince women to go out with him. He was the 20th president at a time when nobody really cared whether you lived or died. He was assassinated in a train station. Think about that. He was killed, in a *train station* . . . the President . . . killed . . . in a train station. Oh, the toils of life in the 1800s. Rest in peace, angel.

CHESTER A. ARTHUR

Chester A. Arthur was the culmination of everything US citizens loved in a president. Funny name? Check. Middle initial in his name? Check. Puffy face with a thick mustache and side whiskers? Check. When he put his name on the ballot, it was pretty much over for the other contestants. He was the son of a Baptist preacher and learned the art of expelling demons from poor, wretched souls faster than anyone ever had before. He was casting out so many demons that one newspaper reported that an entire city block's worth of demons were hovering above the city, not knowing where to go. He was unable to use his spiritual powers to save himself from kidney disease, however, and he died in 1886 just as he was up for reelection. We'll see you on those gold streets, Mr. A. Arthur.

GROVER CLEVELAND

Grover Cleveland was the first Democrat elected to office after the end of the Civil War. He was also the first president to leave the White House and return for a second term four years later. He was a tough president who took no favors and didn't hide his disdain for those who sought to upend democracy. This made him relatively unpopular, and he was abandoned by his own party in 1896.

BENJAMIN HARRISON

Benjamin Harrison was only 5'6" and quickly earned the nickname "Little Ben." The Queen would often joke, "We have Big Ben, they have Little Ben." He was one of the first presidents to go on a campaign trail. He would hold "front porch speeches" where he would arouse the nation through spirited rhetoric and lively discussion.

Little Ben was proud of his foreign policy and was dedicated to stealing Hawaii from the native people.

GROVER CLEVELAND

Surprise! It's Grover Cleveland again. Grover Cleveland allegedly forgot to get some personal belongings and furniture from the White House after his first term expired, and was not allowed back in due to Benjamin Harrison's raging little man syndrome, so Grover had to run for president again in order to retrieve his belongings. Thank goodness he won and was able to retrieve his things because he had terrible taste in interior design.

WILLIAM MCKINLEY

William McKinley was the 25th President of the United States and the man responsible for beating the heck out of Spain in the Spanish-American War. He loved Spanish women and hated to do it, but deep down in his heart he knew he also loved war. He ultimately flipped a coin and decided he would declare war if it landed on heads. It landed on tails, but he flipped it again, citing "interference with the wind." This time it landed on heads, and the rest is history. He was also assassinated. A lot of presidents were assassinated. Seems like distrust in the government runs deep?

THEODORE ROOSEVELT

Theodore Roosevelt was the first certified bad-boy president of the 20th century, reigning from 1901 to 1909.

Being the youngest president in history, he was often called "baby face Teddy" by his constituents. To this he replied, "Would a baby wrestle lions in the Amazon rainforest?" When he returned from the Amazon, he learned that his wife and mother had died. This was very sad for Theodore, and he fled to South Dakota to learn to ride horsies and capture outlaws (America was still pretty rough and tumble in the early 1900s). After leaving the White House, he began his long and prosperous life as a tour guide at the Natural History Museum in New York City, making an appearance in *Night at the Museum,* a great movie about sentient museum taxidermies.

WILLIAM HOWARD TAFT

"Free Willy," as he was called by his nudist colony buddies, was the only person to be both president and chief justice of the Supreme Court. He got so sick and tired of dealing with the Supreme Court's ridiculous laws against public nudity that he decided to take matters into his own hands, literally. He was the president when the *Titanic* sank, and tragically lost his friend Archibald Butts in the sinking. He delivered the eulogy, famously saying, "Losing Butts was like losing a brother." This was an ironic thing to say being that Taft was a big-time nudist.

WOODROW WILSON

Woodrow Wilson was the 28th President of the United States and the man responsible for the rise of Adolf

Hitler. After World War I he enacted the Treaty of Versailles, which imposed harsh and unfair reparations on Germany, which Hitler used to manipulate the German people into thinking they had been ripped off. It wasn't intentional, and while we *do* forgive Woodrow, sadly he will always be known as the man with a really odd first name who basically laid out the red carpet for Adolf.

WARREN G. HARDING

Warren Harding was our 29th president at a time when America was recovering from World War I. After a lot of "teeth pulling," as Warren liked to say, he was able to get the stock markets to start performing better, which in turn made him look better. This was good for the country, of course, but let's just say there were a lot of toothless stockbrokers on Wall Street. This continued for about two years until word started to spread about Warren Harding's friends using his office for their own personal gain. This did not sit well with "ol' Hardball," as his childhood nanny called him, and he began to take his friends on "retreats" to "special islands" near Cuba that rhyme with "Flontonomo Bay" where he would "ask them" what they were secretly doing. Let's just say he didn't like what they told him. He died in 1923 of a heart attack.

CALVIN COOLIDGE

At 2:30 a.m., August 3rd, 1923, while visiting Vermont, Calvin Coolidge received word that he was president.

By the light of a kerosene lamp, his father, who was a notary public, administered the oath of office as Coolidge placed his hand on the family Bible. Coolidge became our first "normal-looking guy" to be president. His nose was pointy and his lips a bit pursed, but he made do with what God gave him. For the next six years, he worked to build America into what it was always meant to be, a glittering megacity with gold streets and Henry Ford yammering on in the papers about how "not enough idiots are buying my Model A!" Calvin died in 1933 and his last words were, "This Depression has got to go!"

HERBERT HOOVER

Herbert Hoover was the 31st president and a man known for two things: having a potty mouth and being clinically depressed. His wife called him "Ol' Sore Eyes" due to the immense Hefty XL-size trash bags that began to appear under his eyes due to his crippling depression. When onlookers would see him, they would grimace and shelter their children from the sight of the man, which would send Hoover on a ten-minute cursing rant, earning him the nickname "Hoover Damn." It only took a few months of his presidency for his sad presence to rub off on the entire country, and on October 29th, 1929, the United States entered the Great Depression. Many blamed Hoover for this calamity. When he wasn't cursing or throwing a depressed tantrum, he was often seen standing naked on the White House lawn, challenging the local high school boys to a game of "who can cry the longest." Herbert was a sad, sad man and not a great president. Not bad-looking, though. He had a decent physique, noted one of the high schoolers.

FRANKLIN ROOSEVELT

Franklin Roosevelt was nothing more than a really, really, really, *really* great president. He was such a great president that we forgive him for basically being dictator of America for over a decade as he usurped the term limits put in place by the Founding Fathers. His wife, Eleanor, once said that "My husband has such a desire to be King of America that I swear if he wasn't such a good lover, I would have to agree with him." Franklin saved America during the Great Depression, and singlehandedly took on Adolf Hitler in World War II. Franklin even challenged Hitler to a game of chess, to which Hitler replied, "I would never play chess with someone in a wheelchair, it wouldn't be fair." To this Franklin replied, "What on god's green earth are you on about? My mind isn't gone, just my legs!" At which point every member of Congress stood up and roared with laughter, one of them even falling down and needing to be carted off the House floor. Franklin was a really great president, and if he was smart, he would've found indigenous land and chiseled his face into the face of a cliff, but oh well. We're just left with his beautiful face on pictures and postcards, which is good enough for me, trust me.

HARRY TRUMAN

Harry "A-bomb" Truman was our 33rd president and the one responsible for dropping the atomic bombs on Hiroshima and Nagasaki, killing thousands of innocent civilians. He was also known for having an ungodly amount of body hair. His real name was actually "Harrison," but the nickname "Harry" was given to him during one of his famous "White House sponge bath speeches," where he would take a sponge bath while delivering the State of the Union. One of Truman's constituents said of him: "He had a corset-like device he would wear under his suits that would tame the grizzly-bear amount of hair growing on his body. It was really, really uncomfortable to see him without clothes on." Harry Truman took a vacation to Oregon in the early fifties, and to this day is credited as being the real reason the myth surrounding "Bigfoot" began. My oh my, he was hairy.

DWIGHT EISENHOWER

Dwight Eisenhower was the supreme Allied commander in Europe during World War II and a man known for wearing those cool aviator glasses around everywhere. He wore them so much, in fact, that the Capitol building had to install five times as many lights so he could see where he was going, due to his vision being heavily darkened by the polarized lenses. He was also the first president to broadcast a speech in color on television, which is pretty cool I guess. You know what's not cool? Dwight was the president responsible for greenlighting the bird surveillance program. It's sad that Dwight felt the need to rid our great country of its feathered friends, forever altering history, and leaving his mark as one of the worst men to ever live.

JOHN F. KENNEDY

Where do I begin? John Fitzgerald Kennedy was our 35th president and the only bird-drone-era president to stand up to the CIA. He told Allen Dulles, "If you don't shut down this operation, I will put your head on a spike on top of the Washington Monument!" He believed in freedom, justice, and liberty for all, and was appalled when he found out what was happening behind his back with the bird robots. It's been said that the first time he heard what was happening, he vomited for 36 straight hours, leaving his beautiful wife Marilyn Monroe to clean up after him, to which he said to her, "My god, woman, you're not supposed to be doing that! Leave that for the dogs to clean up." At which point his 12 dogs ran in and started licking up all the vomit, at which point Marilyn was so disgusted that she also vomited, which only made Kennedy vomit more. Three days later he was dead in Dallas, allegedly due to Lee Harvey Oswald's gunshot wound to the head. This is a blatant lie. He was killed by the CIA for trying to stop bird drone surveillance. Rest in peace, John. We love you.

LYNDON B. JOHNSON

Here we go again: another totally out-of-left-field first name for a president . . . but that didn't stop Lyndon from taking credit for all of JFK's legislation! LBJ had a wife, and do you know what her name was? Lady "Bird" Johnson! Yeah, that's right. This was a time in American history when the overlords loved to shove it down our throats and laugh in our face, mocking our inability to stop the bird genocide from happening. Lady Bird Johnson was a terrible lady on account of the fact that she personally killed over 2,350 birds with a shotgun out the back of the White House's East Wing. Lyndon (crazy name) would watch her and laugh, often yelling at the White House servants to bring him more lollipops, which he would suck while he watched his wife's hideous hobby. He was also responsible for escalating the Vietnam War and is known for being basically a really bad president. Nothing could save this country, though, because—spoiler alert—presidential integrity doesn't get much better from here.

RICHARD NIXON

Richard Nixon is one of my favorite presidents. Want to know why? Well, if you use your brain, it's obvious! He was a really pathetic man and, yes, this was funny, but it's not why he's one of my favorites. Yes, he was also incredibly ugly, and it still makes me laugh just thinking about his Pinocchio nose, but that's not why he's one of my favorites, either. He's one of my favorites because he was so careless with his actions as president that he was caught talking about bird drone surveillance in public over 25 times! The "official narrative" on Watergate is that Nixon was caught spying on members of the Democratic party, but this isn't the full story. Want to know why it's called "Watergate"? Because Operation: *Water* the Country had officially been exposed, and the first news story that ran about Nixon's bird robot plan had been called "Watergate"? in reference to it. Obviously the elites did not like that their entire plan had been found out, so they quickly suicided everyone who knew, including prominent journalists and anyone who spoke in favor of exposing Nixon and the government. They then carefully crafted a fake narrative about some building complex named Watergate, and the rest is history. Fake history, but history nonetheless. Nixon was a bad president, super ugly.

GERALD FORD

After Richard Nixon was caught and impeached, public confidence in the government was sorely lacking. It's been said that in 1975, over 76% of the public wanted to abolish the democratic system and impose a "King of America" situation. The elites did not like this. They needed someone with a strong American backbone to take the reins of the country and reestablish pseudo trust. So, they tapped one of America's good ol' boys, Gerald Ford. Having founded the Ford Motor Company, he was a staple of American ingenuity and represented everything America stood for. He should've stuck to cars, however, because he was totally out of his element. He didn't even know the capital of America was in Washington, DC, and he showed up in New York City on his first day in office. He wasn't super ugly; compared to Nixon he was actually quite good-looking.

JIMMY CARTER

James Earl Carter Jr. is an American former politician who served as the 39th President of the United States from 1977 to 1981. A member of the Democratic Party, he previously served as the 76th governor of Georgia from 1971 to 1975, and as a Georgia state senator from 1963 to 1967.

RONALD REAGAN

Ronald Reagan was the first and last president to have also worked as a celebrity in Hollywood. It's ironic that we would allow someone who pretends to be other people to "play president" for eight years. It was cute watching him try to pretend that he knew what he was doing, or where the light switch was in the Oval Office. He was just really dumb! And really old, not that I have anything against old people; I love them. They're the best. But when this old person is systematically murdering bluebirds and blackbirds and redbirds and greenbirds by the millions, you have to admit to yourself that enough is enough—this guy has to go! Ronald Reagan was one bad president.

GEORGE H. W. BUSH

"Big Bush," as he was called by his wife, Barbara, had the smile of a crow and the nose of a hound dog. It's been said that he could sniff out real birds from three miles away, at which point he would shoot them, and Barb would run after them on all fours like a hunting dog. This sounds cute, but it was really quite terrifying to watch, according to one White House intern who was responsible for cleaning out George's nose with a Q-tip so he could smell better. He had a few kids, most notably Jeb and George. Jeb is a sweet fellow who really just wanted to be like his papa. Sadly, he was really quite dumb and couldn't ever remember which room his dad slept in, so he was unable to see his dad. It's been said by someone close to the family that Jeb once went 18 months without seeing "daddy"; he was wandering the halls of the White House, blissfully unaware that he wasn't even *in* the White House—he was in a boarding school. George H. W. Bush was a tall man of noble build, but obviously hated birds like most post-Eisenhower presidents did, so we hate him.

BILL CLINTON

Bill Clinton was our 42nd president and a man of great conviction. Conviction for wasting his time playing the saxophone instead of shutting down the bird surveillance operation! Obviously at this point you see that this is not getting any better. In fact, I am in a total rage while writing this. The fact that I even have to write about the bird robot agenda enrages me. You would think more people would wake up to this. I am sick and tired of trying to wake this country up! When will our common sense return! Have you seen a baby pigeon? No! Wake up! Think for yourself! Oh my goodness, I am so sick of this nightmare! Bill was a pretty good-looking guy. Bad president.

GEORGE W. BUSH

George W. Bush is a man who needs no introduction. Ever been to a Cracker Barrel? You've met George Bush. Ever seen a Ford F-350 flying down the highway going 25 over the speed limit? You've met George Bush. We've all met George Bush in one way or another. Apparently he's a painter now, that's cute. He should paint a picture of himself being thrown over the side of a pirate ship because if I ever found myself on a pirate ship with him I would definitely make him walk the plank. Ever heard of the Patriot Act? Yeah, thought so. That was George Bush's idea. It made bird surveillance legal. Yeah, totally legal. Even if they admit what they're doing, technically it's legal. That's insane! When will people learn that these old men do not care about anything other than furthering the bird drone crisis in this country? George was decently attractive.

BARACK OBAMA

Where to begin? He spent his entire eight years in office doing everything but shutting down bird drone surveillance. Literally everything. He threw first pitches, went on the *Tonight Show* with that rat Jimmy Fallon, ate crumpets with that old bag the Queen, etc. But he didn't bat an eye at the over 12 billion birds that were murdered. Obviously he didn't want to be JFK'd, but come on man, have a backbone. Obama was a very good-looking guy, but a terrible president. He was such a good-looking guy that I'm almost inclined to let him slide a bit, because at this point what could he even do?

He was actually hot. No, sexy. I would let Obama . . . let's just say Obama is a good-looking guy but a terrible, terrible president. He's also from Hawaii, which Benjamin Harrison stole from the natives, so he's implicated in that theft as well. Why hasn't he been arrested? Because America is one big land of hypocrisy.

DONALD TRUMP

Oh boy. I was waiting for this one. Donald Trump was a famous businessman who became president after he convinced half the country that he was one cool guy, but in reality, he was nothing more than a big chunkhead parading around with his ridiculously good-looking family, sucking the blood of the American people and leaving us with the bill. He didn't do a thing to stop bird drone surveillance and even attempted to construct a wall that would've had radar deflectors to keep out real birds from Mexico. This guy was bad, bad. And very ugly! My goodness. The contrast between him and Obama is stark. I bet you're expecting me to tell you that he contracted pumpkinhead from exposure to bird poison early in life. Nope! Sure, it'd be an easy thing to imply, but it just didn't happen. And I'm not in the business of making up a bunch of stuff about various presidents for laughs—this book is about telling the *truth*!

JOE BIDEN

Joseph Biden is the current president at the time of this writing, and while he currently hasn't done anything to shut down bird drone surveillance, I'll give him the benefit of the doubt and hold my tongue until he's proven guilty. After all, maybe he's secretly shutting down the robots behind closed doors? Probably not, but Joseph . . . please. If you are reading this, I beg you. Please. I am literally on my knees. I just got on my knees. Please shut down the birds. Please. Oh god please, Joe, we need the real birds back. You're a cool guy, I love your sunglasses! They are a great look on your face. They complement your masculine facial structure. Please shut down the birds. Do it for the children. Do it for all those who have never heard the beautiful song of a bluebird on a Saturday morning. Do it for all those who have never seen a lark swoop down over the fog on a winter morning. Do it because it's the right thing to do. You are very sexy. Please, I beg you. Deactivate the bird robots.

6

BIRD BRAIN

**HOW THE DEEP STATE USES PROPAGANDA
IN THE MEDIA TO BRAINWASH THE MASSES**

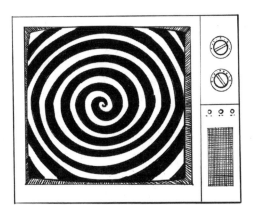

The government and the media have been carefully programming your brain using propaganda ever since you were a little baby. The process of *undoing* brainwashing (known as deprogramming) is difficult and requires the expertise of a well-educated professional, but I will try anyway.

Before reading this book, you probably liked birds. Many people do (there are millions of people in the United States who count "birdwatching" as one of their hobbies, completely unaware that the birds are watching them back). At *worst* you were probably neutral about birds. These positive feelings you have toward birds are not your own feelings at all. You've been socially conditioned to feel the way you do. The elite overlords who benefit from bird surveillance the most feed you pro-bird ideology to keep you numb to the constant presence of birds (or really, bird *drones*) in your life. To make you trust—and maybe even *love*—these birds. To keep you from asking questions. This is why you're so bombarded with bird imagery.

Think about it—bird imagery is ubiquitous in the media. You see it in corporate logos. Anthropomorphic bird characters saturate children's entertainment. Allusions to birds are common in fiction and in songwriting. Bird symbolism is even baked right into our national identity. What's the symbol of American independence? The eagle. The cruel irony is that nothing represents your LACK of freedom more than a bird! It's like they're making fun of us. These people are so sick.

In order to undo the brainwashing that's been done to you, you have to be aware of the propaganda all around you, so let's examine the pervasiveness of bird imagery in American culture and what it all means.

BIRD IMAGERY IN CORPORATE BRANDING

Many large corporations in the US know about the bird surveillance operation, and they support it completely. Why? The answer is simple: data collection.

We all know that large corporations track your Internet activity so that they can market products to you. That's no secret. Selling ads is how social media websites and search engines make their money. The more they know about you, the more ads they can sell you. But what you *don't* know is that they monitor your activity in *real* life, too. There are many large corporations in the US that have access to the video feeds from the robot drones. They have access to all the archived video as well. We're talking billions and billions of hours of footage, being used for data collection by corporate brands. The federal government is happy to give them this access, because, theoretically, better marketing means a stronger economy.

So, large corporations have good reason to protect the bird surveillance operation, and they're happy to play their part. They do this by incorporating birds into their logos. This helps keep bird imagery completely ubiquitous, keeping you numb to the constant presence of birds.

BIRD IMAGERY IN ENTERTAINMENT

The entertainment industry has its own role to play in normalizing birds. It's important to know that the federal government has a big say in what does and does not get aired on television. Children are often the targets of pro-bird propaganda in entertainment. There are tons of cartoon bird characters in children's entertainment. These characters are usually depicted as sweet and innocent. How many "bad guy" bird characters can you think of? Almost zero. Once again, this is all a part of the propaganda machine conditioning us to trust birds implicitly.

Let's talk about the worst offender of all. "Big Bird" is a government psyop designed to endear birds to young children. He has become the quintessential "nice" bird character in popular children's entertainment. Because we grow up learning things from Big Bird, we start to see him (and by extension, *all* birds) as a gentle authority figure. Someone we can trust and shouldn't question.

THE FIRST LADY RITE OF PASSAGE

It's become a sick tradition for politicians and other important cultural figures to make the trip to Sesame Street to "kiss the ring" of Big Bird. In recent years,

American presidents have delegated this job to the First
Lady. Here's a fun game: go online and see how many
pictures you can find of former First Ladies posing with
Big Bird. It's a *lot*.

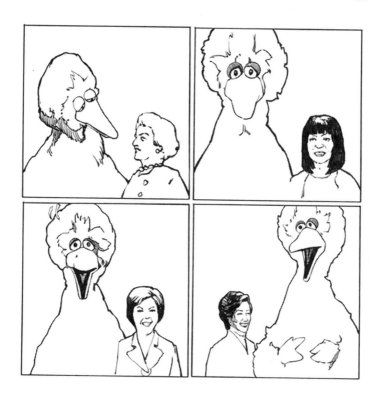

THANKSGIVING: NOT WHAT IT SEEMS

America is a country that loves its traditions. Fireworks on the Fourth of July, shopping on Black Friday, football on Sunday, etc. Traditions like these are important. Unfortunately, the Deep State has manufactured a few traditions of their own, ones that push their sinister bird agenda. It is shocking how quickly and easily this country accepted **ritualized bird worship** as a normal part of life.

Let's talk Thanksgiving. It's *supposed* to be a time where we all get together to be thankful for what we've been given, but it's *actually* a fake holiday created by the Deep State to advance pro-bird ideology. It is a gigantic ceremonial brainwashing activity. Still feeling "thankful"? Because you shouldn't.

Let's think long and hard about what you do every Thanksgiving . . .

YOU WAKE UP BRIGHT AND EARLY TO WATCH THE ALL-MIGHTY BIRD SOARING ABOVE THE STREETS LIKE SOME SORT OF GOD

YOU PLACE BIRD IDOLS IN YOUR HOME—A SYMBOLIC INVITATION TO BIRDS EVERYWHERE TO COME WATCH YOU AND LISTEN TO YOU AT YOUR MOST PRIVATE MOMENTS

YOU GATHER AROUND AND PRAY TO THE BIRD

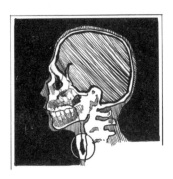

THEN YOU EAT THE BIRD, CONSUMING THE BIOTRACKING TECHNOLOGY THAT THE GOVERNMENT PLACES IN EVERY THANKSGIVING "TURKEY." THE LIE BECOMES A PART OF YOU. YOU LITERALLY *SWALLOW* IT!

THE PRESIDENTIAL TURKEY PARDON

Perhaps the most revolting display of propaganda is the annual pardoning of the Thanksgiving turkey. This sick tradition began during the presidency of George H. W. Bush and continues to this day. Every November, the sitting president ceremonially "pardons" a live turkey, thus saving it from being slaughtered and eaten. As we know, every US president since Eisenhower (except JFK) is complicit in bird genocide.

The annual pardoning of the turkey is a lazy bit of propaganda that's supposed to make it look like the government cares about birds. It's so on-the-nose that it's almost comical. And yet, every November, the media swarms the White House to watch another turkey be pardoned. How much more gullible could we be?

CHRISTMAS: A TEST OF WHAT THE IDIOT MASSES ARE WILLING TO BELIEVE

Thanksgiving isn't the only holiday hiding a grim secret. Christmas is one of the biggest and darkest lies in the history of mankind! This cozy winter "holiday" is barely a holiday at all—it's a test of what the average idiot such as yourself is willing to believe. The government has been testing the waters in this way for centuries. Slowly pushing bigger and bigger lies on the masses in order to see how stupid we really are.

It turns out we're pretty damn stupid. The whole idea of "Christmas" was designed by the government, and it was designed to be as *absurd* as possible. They knew that if they could make us go along with something as ridiculous as Christmas, then we'd go along with *anything*. In many ways, the Christmas psyop was a precursor to bird surveillance. It was a test to see if we'd be stupid enough to let bird surveillance happen without questioning anything.

Let's open up our minds and think about how nonsensical the holiday is. We sit around a pine tree—which we've dragged into our home for some reason—and eat candy out of a sock while we wait for an immortal man from the uninhabitable North Pole to climb down our chimney and leave us gifts. All the while, we sing nonsense phrases like "Ho ho ho!" and "Fa la la la la." Do we ever question these traditions? Nope! We just accept them as a way of life. The same way we never question birds. We just accept them as "real," even though they're not.

"THE 12 DAYS OF CHRISTMAS" IS A GOVERNMENT BRAINWASHING SONG!

Half the days are about birds no one has ever heard of! What is a partridge? What is a French hen?? A turtle-dove? WHAT THE HELL IS A TURTLEDOVE?!

THE REAL-LIFE DEATH TOLL OF CHRISTMAS

There are even *darker* truths to the Christmas holiday. Yes, it's a government psyop to make you stupid, but it has also done real-life harm. What if I told you the US government killed Santa?

Kristopher Kringle

It's true. When the government dropped the poison toxins that killed the bird population, they accidentally killed several caribou (sometimes called reindeer) owned by "Santa," the local nickname of a Montana rancher whose real name was Kristopher Kringle. The government-created bird poison was not supposed to kill other species of animals, but in very rare cases it had a lethal effect on caribou. Kris was devastated, because his livestock was his livelihood. He began alerting other ranchers in the area to the strange toxins that were killing his reindeer. He also began reaching out to people in local government in Montana, demanding to know what was going on. Where were these strange toxins coming from?

Well, the government does not like when people *demand answers*. At some point in the early 1970s, Kris Kringle was kidnapped by the government and sent to Guantanamo Bay. He is presumed to be long dead.

7

A MOVEMENT IS BORN

THE CASE FOR HOPE

After hearing about all these atrocities committed by your very own Uncle Sam, you may be feeling terrified, lost, and hopeless. Like a withered shell of a person. And not a beautiful conch shell, but a gross barnacle clam shell. It can be easy to fall into despair and lose all semblance of your humanity. Just sleepwalking through your life

The face of hope

from one part-time job to another, constantly searching for your next "hit" to distract you from what the government did . . .

Well, I want to give you a little gift: the gift of hope. I'd like you to look me in my eyes (use the picture to the left) while I tell you this: everything is going to be okay. It's never too late to fight back as long as you have **hope**. Hope is what got the original Birds Aren't Real activists out on the streets back in the 1970s. At this point I'd like to tell you the story of those original Birds Aren't Real activists. We have to learn from our elders if we ever want to become effective bird surveillance activists ourselves. They gave us the blueprint we needed to construct the skyscraper of change. So without further ado, this is the story of the original Birds Aren't Real movement. They believed that the world could be changed for the better. So do I, and after reading this, hopefully so will you. Let's draw as much inspiration as we can from these brave warriors of truth.

WHO WAS CLARK GRIFFIN?

Clark Griffin

CLARK GRIFFIN is considered the original founder of the Birds Aren't Real movement. He was responsible for the "Great Awakening" of 1975. That's when the fight against bird surveillance all began.

Clark was born in San Francisco in 1955. He was interested in politics from a very early age and became an avid political activist. When he was only eight years old,

Clark helped organize a teachers' strike at his public elementary school. By age ten, he was regularly attending anti-Vietnam marches. As a teen, he would often stand outside CIA headquarters with a megaphone and demand "full transparency."

Neither his local government nor the federal government liked Clark Griffin very much. He was a thorn in their side with his constant protesting and rallying. But there was *one* man in government who saw Clark Griffin as an ally. That man's name was Eugene Price, a CIA operative who had the courage to do the right thing and blow the whistle on Operation: Water the Country.

THE WHISTLEBLOWER

In the cold marble hallways of history, we are often beckoned to gaze upon such greats as Teddy Roosevelt, or Eleanor Roosevelt, or Franklin Roosevelt. But one man deserves to be praised above them all, and that man is **EUGENE PRICE.**

Eugene was a man who joined the CIA in 1957, hoping to serve his country. He was a proud patriot and he

Eugene Price

truly believed that the CIA was doing good things. He was shocked when he got there and found out all the insane and illegal stuff they were up to, particularly the fact that they were releasing bird drones by the thousands. But for years, Eugene stayed quiet. That was just how things were at the CIA. You were expected to stay quiet. Eugene's boss would reinforce this principle by looking Eugene in the eyes at the end of every workday and asking, "What did you see here today?" To which Eugene would reply, "Nothing."

This was his life until 1974, when he experienced something that very few CIA agents have ever experienced: a visit from his conscience. One day he was eating his lunch on a park bench a few blocks from CIA headquarters when he noticed a gorgeous family taking a stroll through the grass, looking up at the sky and admiring the white fluffy clouds that signified the end of summer. Eugene watched the happy family for a few minutes, thinking about his *own* family. Just then, he noticed a pigeon following this family in the park, and he knew it was gathering data. He had a sudden vision of fire and brimstone coming down from the sky like hellfire. He became overwhelmed with emotion and threw himself to the ground, screaming in agony as the weight of his actions hit him like a bag of Soros bricks.

Maybe you've been in a similar situation, one where you were overcome with guilt for your actions. I know I have. One time when I was seven, this old lady that lived next door gave me a dirty look so I threw a handful of rocks at her car. I don't feel good about it, and sometimes I feel the urge to find her and go apologize, so I know what Eugene was going through that day. The weight of your actions can be a lot sometimes.

Do *you* have anything you feel guilty for? Write

about it here. This is for your eyes only. Just find a pen and let your conscience be your guide.

_____

_____

_____

_____

_____

_____

_____

_____

_____

_____

_____

_____

_____

Doesn't it feel good to release your pain onto paper and revel in the afterglow of a spotless conscience? This is what Eugene did in 1975 when he decided to expose the government's bird surveillance program.

THE AWAKENING

> *"I wish it need not have happened in my time,"*
> *said Frodo. "So do I," said Gandalf, "and so do*
> *all who live to see such times. But that is not for*
> *them to decide. All we have to decide is what to*
> *do with the time that is given us."*

When Eugene decided it was time to leak the truth about bird surveillance, he thought of Clark Griffin, the charismatic young activist who used to yell through a megaphone outside of CIA headquarters.

A soft rain fell quietly on the cobblestone streets one September night in 1975. The distant wailing of a police siren reverberated against the stone facade of one particular building that sat on the corner of the street. Inside, 25-year-old Clark Griffin was hunched over a granite countertop eating a bowl of cereal, half-awake, half-asleep. At that moment a knock came from the front door and Clark stopped chewing and looked over his shoulder, wondering who could possibly need his presence at that ungodly hour.

Dropping his spoon into the bowl, he yawned and opened the front door. He was surprised to see that there was not a person at his door, but rather a wooden box. Clark brought it inside and stared at it for a few minutes before finally grabbing a hammer and prying off the lid. From this moment on, his life would be forever defined by the contents of this unexpected package. Just as he opened that box, his phone rang. "Hello?" Clark asked, feeling uneasy. The voice on the other end was soft as it replied, "Clark, my name is Eugene. You have just been given sole possession of a box which contains evidence of a national conspiracy of unparalleled magnitude. I am trusting you with this information. Please don't let the country down. People need to know the contents of that box. I believe you can do this. Please don't fail us."

Clark began asking questions of the mysterious caller, but he only received this enigmatic reply: "I can't say any more. You will never hear my voice again." Just like that, the call ended.

THE BOX

Clark was still stunned as he began to dig through this mysterious box. It was full of documents and tapes pertaining to the CIA's bird surveillance operation. It was all the evidence anyone could need to prove that the government had killed off the birds and was replacing them with surveillance drones.

As Clark familiarized himself with the contents of **THE BOX**, as it was affectionately called by others, he slowly became "awake." Becoming "awake" is a rite of passage for Bird Truthers, something that only happens once you've fully crossed the river of doubt into the land of truth. The river of doubt takes many forms, the most common being, "How could this have happened? How could the government have done this? That is preposterous!"

I beg of you, dear friend, **cross the river.** Once you do this and admit to yourself that the United States government *has* done bad things and *is* evil, we can begin our work.

Clark began his work by studying every single piece of evidence Eugene had put into The Box. Blueprints for the first bird robots. Maps of where power lines would go in certain cities. Letters from high-ranking CIA officers detailing the progress of the "great removal" of birds. With each document, Clark became increasingly aware of his surroundings. One day he noticed a parrot perched outside his window in Philadelphia, staring right at him. As you've learned in the Bird Drone Field Guide, parrots are linguistic analysts who read lips and send the data back to the Pentagon. Clark pulled the curtains closed. From now on, they would remain that way.

Before I continue, imagine with me a world where the information in this book is public knowledge. Imagine a world where the education system teaches the truth of what has gone on in our "Land of the Free." The window is beginning to close, my friend. What was started by Eugene's guilty conscience and continued by Clark Griffin is quickly becoming a long-forgotten legend. Nobody believes anything I say anymore. It used to be that I could walk up to people on the street corner and begin telling them that there was a bird 35 feet away in a tree tracking them, and they would look at me terrified and walk away. I knew I was doing the lord's work. Now, people laugh in my face and call me names. I don't mind the name-calling. I got used to it in high school. What I *do* mind is the lack of open minds in this country. Nobody seems to accept the reality that they might not know everything. They just hear me say "birdwatching goes both ways" and they laugh in my face. I can only imagine what *Clark* felt as he told people about the bird surveillance crisis.

BIRDS AREN'T REAL!

TRUTH TOUR

THE MOVEMENT BEGINS

The events that took place between 1975 and 1977 changed the course of our entire country. People often ask me what time period I would visit if time travel was possible. I always say, "I would want to be with Clark Griffin in those early days of the Birds Aren't Real movement." I want to be there for the sleepless nights and the whispered secret meetings. I want to hear the scurry of footsteps in dark alleyways as we escape the CIA hitmen sent to suicide Bird Truthers on a monthly basis. That's where I want to be.

Here's the thing: back in the seventies there was no official handbook on how to expose the biggest crime ever perpetrated by the US government. Clark Griffin had to invent his own way. The first step was to get the word out. He began traveling from town to town in a beat-up old van and yelling through a megaphone, "BIRDS AREN'T REAL." Most people thought he was crazy. But there were a handful of people who were willing to hear him out and look at the evidence. Over the course of a few months, he had amassed a following of just under 50 people, mostly college students. They became known as the "Fab 50." Clark hated this name and tried to ban it from the movement's vocabulary.

Clark's burgeoning Birds Aren't Real movement continued to grow. Day by day, they made stops at college campuses, town squares, and other highly trafficked spots to pass out pamphlets, tissues, and other helpful materials. Skeptics continued to dismiss, ridicule, and even harass them, but they refused to be silenced. A legendary Washington, DC, rally in 1977 was the first to exceed an attendance of 1,000. This was a huge success for Clark and his team. In just under three years, they had stormed into the musty closet of reality and ripped the light on, revealing Lady Liberty huddled

Opposite: Disrespectful college "news" publication slams the movement.

BIRDBRAINED "ACTIVISTS" TAKE OVER CAMPUS

By Stephen Grier

If you think you've heard it all, get ready for this one. It turns out those winged creatures you see flying through the air every day are not creatures at all. They're robots that the government uses to spy on you. That's what followers of the "Birds Aren't Real" movement think, anyway. And no, they're not joking.

Yesterday morning, over 250 "patriots" swarmed Baylor's campus to preach to students about a government conspiracy dating back to the 1940s. Believers in the Birds Aren't Real conspiracy allege that the bird population was systematically poisoned by the CIA and replaced with robots that are equipped with cameras. They believe the robot birds are used by the government to spy on the American population. Why? Who knows. The angry mob, equipped with megaphones and informative brochures, are a mostly incoherent bunch who have trouble articulating why, exactly, they think the government is spying on them. Their leader, a San Franciscan named Clark Griffin, made vague allusions to "anti-communist measures." Apparently, Clark thinks the government has nothing better to do than battle communism, a political ideology that is largely unpopular in America.

Baylor students were both baffled and amused by Griffin and his tinfoil-hat mob. Several students posed for pictures with the activists, and flipped through their absurd brochures with glee. I was one of them. To Griffin's credit, he does weave quite an exciting tale. One of the brochures treated me to a story of government intrigue, mass genocide, and secret assassinations. The short version goes as follows: in the 1940s, the CIA developed a specialized poison that only affected birds. Working with the Boeing Company, the CIA dispersed this poison across the country from planes, successfully killing off the entirety of the bird population. From there, the government used the media to instigate nuclear fears as an excuse to construct fake fallout shelters around the country. These fake shelters were actually facilities for constructing robotic surveillance birds. Careful—they might be watching you now! And if you're wondering what their proof is, Griffin has plenty of it. The brochure features a bounty of "leaked government information" that was apparently stolen straight from CIA headquarters. Sounds perfectly plausible, right?

The activists, who are in the middle of a a cross-country "Tour of Freedom," were asked to leave by campus security after an hour. Yet another act of authoritarian oppression, I suppose.

While vaguely amusing, yesterday's "Birds Aren't Real" fiasco was a disheartening sight to behold. Baylor is meant to be a place where knowledge is cherished and protected. It should never be an institution that entertains harebrained conspiracy theories. Let's hope the Tour of Freedom has better luck on its next stop, because I for one know my fellow Baylor scholars are not easily swayed by sensationalism and mindless speculation. I hope the same goes for the rest of the country.

in a corner, making out with the devil. People were waking up.

WE LOVE BIRDS

The trees are bare, the sky is great
No more songs to chase the gloom away.
We've lost the beauty of nature's grace
Replaced with robots that watch
our face.

—**SARAH CLARK, 1979**

The poem above tells a heartbreaking story about a woman reeling from the reality that one of nature's greatest gifts is being systematically removed. This is something all of us Bird Truthers have experienced—especially the ones back in the 1970s. A large portion of the Birds Aren't Real movement back then was animal rights activists who were appalled at the blatant mass murder of such a vital part of the ecosystem. "SAVE OUR BIRDS!" they would scream as they marched down the city streets. One bird enthusiast named Andrew Winkley, head of a group called Students United Under Birds (or SUUB), joined the Birds Aren't Real movement in 1976. He has this to say of his experience:

I was just beginning to find my way. I had just graduated high school and moved out of my parents' house. My parents were jerks. I mean they were real jerks. They wouldn't let me do hardly anything and I had no freedom. I couldn't even go to Disney World because "Pluto and Goofy were caricatures of demons sent to indoctrinate" me. I mean, these people were really nuts. If I knew back then what I know now, boy would they get it. I mean I would really lay into them. "You morons!" I would say to them, "I'm gonna send you straight to the looney bin when you turn 80! You won't find me taking care of you!" So I finally move out of the house, and then bam, on my first day of college there's a guy standing on top of a van shouting. So I go over to see what he's yelling about. I assumed it was some commie crap or some junk about the "establishment." But to my surprise he was passing around documents about birds being killed. That really got me riled up. Ever since I was a kid I would spend time in my grandpa's backyard looking at the birds and pointing out different kinds and stuff. My grandpa was blind from using chlorine to clean his glasses, so I had to describe these birds to him. As I learned to describe them, I fell in love with them and their songs. I began to daydream about being in the woods with birds blanketing me in the trees, singing and chirping. And then my dad would storm into my room and throw a bag of trash at me and say, "This is how much trash your generation left on the side of the road today. Are you happy? You and your friends should be ashamed of what you're doing to the world." So when I heard this guy on my campus *saying what the government had been doing, I remembered how much I loved birds. It makes me sad now, especially since Clark is gone. He went missing a few years ago and I guess the government got away with making it happen.*

Everything Andrew said about Clark going missing is sadly true. In 1989, Clark's house was raided by the FBI. All of the materials he had on bird surveillance were confiscated over "national security concerns."

GONE BUT NOT FORGOTTEN

When Clark went missing in the late eighties, he was only 27 years old. His short life came to an abrupt end, all because he was speaking out against the US government. Clark was last seen with his hands behind his head, looking dejected, in the back of a SWAT team van. It's been rumored that he was shipped off to Guantanamo Bay and most likely executed, but we'll never really know for sure what happened to *our* leader. I find it extremely disappointing when I go to a football game and hear the national anthem. What a crock of lies. I always sit down and go "blah blah blah" really loudly. It's very childish but at this point I don't give a damn. I am entirely fed up with the lies and the mainstream media twisting everything we say and do, just like they did to Clark in the 1980s.

Before Clark went missing, he left behind a videotape that was supposed to be aired on prime-time TV. This video was filmed in the Birds Aren't Real campaign office and shows a truly remarkable scene. Clark and many original members of the movement can be seen hard at work, calling senators, designing fliers, and studying the evidence left by Eugene. The tape was discovered by chance at a Goodwill in 2015 and has since been viewed over 500,000 times online since its release by yours truly. My hope is that someone will come forward with more information on Clark, but probably not. It's been a long, painful road for our movement since his departure, but we cling to hope just like our Founding Fathers, who said, "We will not stand for tyranny. We will not stand for Her Royal Highness the Queen playing fiddly sticks with our enemies and using the mainstream media to turn everyone against us. We will rise up like sharks in the waters of time, like *Jaws*. Like the movie *Jaws*."

8

HOW TO HOLD A RALLY

For too long, we have been metaphorically knocking, politely, at the door of our lawmakers—begging to be heard. When the polite knocking didn't work, we started banging our fists—requesting change. That didn't work either. Now, we are done asking nicely. We will come to your city. We will march through your streets. We will come to your front door and instead of knocking we will kick the door down. Bird Truthers will rage through the streets of this nation like floodwater through cracks in the sidewalk. And we will not stop. Not until every bird drone is deactivated and falling from the sky like rain.

—CLARK GRIFFIN, ORIGINAL FOUNDER OF THE
BIRDS AREN'T REAL MOVEMENT

The Deep State tries to make it seem like the Birds Aren't Real movement does not exist. They censor our posts, throw us in jail, and try to intimidate us into staying quiet. But make no mistake: there are thousands of Bird Truthers throughout the country. It's easy to discount numbers on social media, but it's hard to look at hundreds of people swarming the streets and keep thinking that nothing is going on. That's why we hold public demonstrations as often as we can.

In a perfect world, there would be a Bird Truther rally in every single city in the country on every single day of the year, but that can't happen until we get our numbers up. And how do we do that? By rallying. **The #1 way you can help the movement is by holding a Bird Truther rally in your hometown.**

This can be intimidating at first. Hosting a rally is a lot of work, and it can even be dangerous. But don't worry—I've held dozens of rallies over the past few years, and I pretty much have it down to a science by now. There are a few things you can do to make sure that your Birds Aren't Real rally goes down without a hitch. I will explain them all in this section.

Pretty soon, you'll be out there leading a mob of Bird Truthers through the streets, shouting the truth into the faces of thousands of potential new recruits, whether they want to hear it or not.

PREPARATION

When holding a rally, you don't just walk outside and start yelling through a megaphone. While that can be very satisfying, it's not effective. A lot of careful planning must go into this sort of thing if you really want to open the minds of the general public. Before hitting the streets, you'll need to do the following.

ASSEMBLE A TEAM

This is not a one-man job. A rally requires a squadron of five (5) people at minimum to be successful. They are:

1. THE RALLY LEADER

This is the person in charge. The one who will be at the front of the march, leading chants through the megaphone, debating counterprotestors, and generally acting as the "face" of the rally. To be a good Rally Leader is to be an energy composer. They dictate the whole pace and tenor of the rally. They should also be wearing the biggest hat in the group, because this will serve as a visual demonstration of their authority. Personally, I'm partial to a cowboy hat. I usually go with a classic Stetson, but JW Brooks makes a great cowboy hat as well. If you're the Rally Leader, and there's someone at your rally who has a bigger hat, make them take it off.

Typically, the Rally Leader will be a very charismatic person, like myself. I'm definitely a Rally Leader.

2–3. (2) CROWD CONTROL TRUTHERS

A Crowd Control Truther is generally responsible for making sure everyone feels safe and welcome. They conduct the pre-rally assembly, so you can kind of think of them like the "opening act." Once the rally gets started, the CCTs are loosely responsible for keeping things civil. For example, if counterprotestors start to get violent, the CCTs will step in to de-escalate the situation as much as possible. This is a very important job, so it's vital for there to be a minimum of two CCTs. This is a great job for someone not cut out to be a Rally Leader, either because they aren't a confident public speaker or they're not quite good-looking enough.

4. ACTIVISM STATION ATTENDANT

You can't always count on the people attending your rally to bring their own signs and posters. That's why it's a great idea to have a small Activism Station. This can be accomplished with a simple foldout table, large pieces of paper, and several Sharpie markers of all different colors. If a Bird Truther shows up empty-handed, a CCT will escort them to the Activism Station where they can make their own sign before the rally begins. You will need at least one attendant to man the Activism Station. Once the rally begins, the Activism Station Attendant will start passing around informational pamphlets to any citizens who're intrigued by the rally and want to know more about bird surveillance. This is not a good or glamorous job at all but somebody has to do it.

5. THE LOOKOUT

It's VITAL to have one person designated as a lookout. A rally is a prime opportunity for the government to take out as many Bird Truthers as possible. You have no idea how often we find people seriously injured or dead at the end of Birds Aren't Real rallies because they became the victim of a government hummingbird drone (see pg. 65 for more information on hummingbird drones). After a particularly violent rally in 2017 now known as the "Pittsburgh Massacre," we made it mandatory for there to be a Bird Truther on lookout duty at each rally. They are responsible for watching out for attack drones, or any other ways the government might be trying to assassinate our marchers. The Lookout should also be trained in first aid because a lot of marchers faint or suffer heat stroke from the emotional and physical intensity of a rally. Due to the vigilance of our Lookouts, I'm proud to say we have not had anyone die at a Birds Aren't Real rally in over three weeks.

PICK A LOCATION, DATE, AND TIME

Now that you've assembled your team, it's time to choose a location and get a date on the books. Remember, a rally is supposed to be disruptive. You don't want things to get violent but you *do* want to rock the boat. If your rally isn't causing some serious disruptions then no one will pay attention to it and you won't have any leverage, either. That's why it's best to hold your rally in a crowded outdoor location where there is a lot of foot traffic.

The likely best choice of location is the downtown area of your nearest city. The ideal time is on the weekend or on a holiday—any time that a lot of people are off work and trying to enjoy a nice day outside. Ideally, your rally should make it hard for anyone to walk or even access stores or restaurants. That way, there's nothing for people to do *but* watch your rally. Do not be afraid to really ruin people's weekends. As long as they're paying attention, your rally is successful.

PREPARE YOUR MATERIALS

Now that you have a team, a location, and a time, you're ready to prepare your informational materials. Remember, the whole point of this rally is to spread awareness and recruit more Bird Truthers. You need to be prepared for the moment that an interested citizen comes up to you mid-rally and says, "You seem smart. Where can I learn more?" You should always bring an EXCESSIVE amount of informational materials to hand out. That includes Birds Aren't Real pamphlets, posters, and perhaps even this book, as long as you're *absolutely certain* that you aren't talking to a fed.

THE BIG DAY

It's time. The day of the big rally. You've done all the prep work and now you're ready to hit the streets and capture some hearts and minds. To convert mindless sheep into anti-bird-surveillance warriors. Here's how to do it . . .

CREATE AN ASSEMBLY POINT

Your two CCTs should be the first points of contact for everyone attending your rally. Thirty minutes before the rally is scheduled to start, have them plant a large flag at your starting location that says TRUTH WARRIORS

ASSEMBLE HERE. Make sure the flag is flying high enough to be visible from a distance. At this same time, your designated Lookout person should be settling into their lookout spot. This should be somewhere very high up, like the top of a skyscraper.

GREET YOUR MARCHERS

As people start to gather for the rally, have your CCTs greet them and make sure they're prepared. This is the point where the CCTs should be directing people to the Activism Station if they've arrived without signs. Aside from that, the CCTs should be checking in with people to make sure they're mentally ready for what's about to happen. They should be prepared to give pep talks to anyone who is feeling nervous about the rally. You want the pre-rally energy to be high. People should be going into this with excitement and optimism, not fear or doubt. If anyone is feeling nervous about government assassination (which is a fair concern) the CCTs should remind them that there is a designated Lookout overseeing the rally and that they are armed.

THE LEADER ARRIVES

A few minutes before the designated start time, the Rally Leader should arrive in a large vehicle such as a van or truck. This should be a big moment. The marchers are looking to the Rally Leader to project an aura of strength. You don't want your Rally Leader to be too *flashy,* but they should make a strong impression and immediately establish themselves as a dominant person. That's why it's important for him (or her!) to arrive in a very large vehicle. I usually arrive in a van.

THE OPENING SPEECH

Now it's time for the Rally Leader to deliver a rousing speech. This should be done from the top of the large vehicle they rode in on. The goal here is to get the energy up as much as possible. Your marchers should feel like they're about to storm the gates!

Often the opening speech isn't so much a "speech" as it is a series of yelling-based activities. It's always effective to begin with a call-and-response. For example, your Rally Leader can yell through the megaphone, "WHEN I SAY 'STOP THE' YOU SAY 'LIES.' STOP THE . . ." and then everyone yells, "LIES." It feels really good for people to yell.

After several minutes of call-and-response, it's good to switch over to a chant. Keep it simple: "BIRDS AREN'T REAL! BIRDS AREN'T REAL!" The Leader should have the entire crowd worked up by now. You want the energy so high that it feels like the entire crowd is about to explode at any moment.

MOMENT OF SILENCE

Time to bring the energy down completely. The Leader should now lead the crowd in a three-minute moment of silence to pay tribute to the billions of birds that the government has massacred. If you're the Rally Leader, remember to take off your cowboy hat for this.

It may seem strange to bring the energy down so suddenly, but trust me, it works. The sudden emotional whiplash is very effective in awakening an even *deeper* level of energy to be expelled later. In fact, it's good to keep the mood constantly fluctuating throughout the entire rally. I have even pinpointed the perfect "emotional structure" for a rally, which dictates the optimal time to shift the energy and by how much. I have included it on the next page.

BRING IN THE BAGPIPER

At this point the bagpiper will come out and play for several minutes.

MAKE EVERYONE MAD

Now it's time to rapidly shift the energy again. The Rally Leader should suddenly become very angry and encourage the crowd to do the same. Remind the crowd how MAD they should be about bird surveillance! Remind them that they are VICTIMS! Another call-and-response is effective here. Call out, "ARE YOU READY TO FIGHT BACK?" Everyone should respond, "Yes!" Get another chant going: "NO MORE DRONES! NO

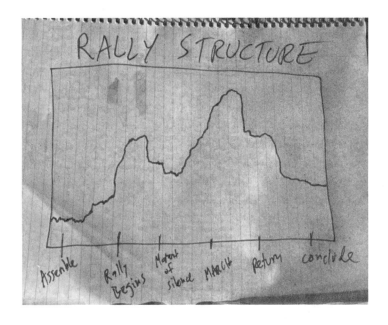

MORE DRONES!" Carry on like this for several minutes. At this point the energy in the crowd will be so high that it's nearly unbearable. Just as everyone is reaching feverish levels of anger, suddenly . . .

IT'S TIME TO MARCH!
The Rally Leader should abruptly begin to march. All of the energy that's been built up should be unleashed on the streets like a pot of water boiling over. Just like that, the rally has begun.

Remember to keep the rally civil and nonviolent. The shadow government often sends in undercover counter-protestors to rile up the crowd and try to instigate violence. They are just doing this to sabotage the rally and make the movement look bad. Never become violent, no matter how much it seems like someone is asking for it. The CCTs should actively be watching out for tense encounters and stepping in to de-escalate.

Your Activism Station Attendant should be passing out pamphlets and other informational materials along the way. The Rally Leader should continue leading chants throughout the entirety of the march. Your Lookout should be watching closely for any assassination attempts. If they do see any assassination attempts, they should blow into a very large whistle to warn people of danger.

• • •

Congratulations! You have now held a successful Birds Aren't Real rally. Hopefully, you've indoctrinated at least a few dozen new recruits into the movement, and ideally no one has been assassinated. If someone *has* been assassinated, try not to be too hard on yourself. It happens.

9

HOW TO OVERTHROW THE US GOVERNMENT

By now it should be pretty clear to you that the United States government is beyond saving. The corruption runs so deep that it has rotted every inch of the system. The only way to fix everything would be to scrap our entire government and start fresh. **To be clear, I fully advocate for a complete overthrow of the government.** This is easier said than done, but it is definitely possible. I have even broken it down into a simple four-step process. What follows is a comprehensive guide to overthrowing the United States government.

STEP 1: FORM A MILITIA

You first need to assemble an army of soldiers. This is something that typically takes a long time. You can really rile people up and appeal to their patriotism as a means of almost manipulating them into feeling like they owe the

Founding Fathers their lives. Say stuff like, "What do you think the Founding Fathers would say if they could see you now, sitting on your couch eating Xxtra Flamin' Hot Cheetos and watching *Pawn Stars* for the fifth time in one day, all while there are billions of bird drones in the sky and elected officials are eating $15,000 caviar on Air Force One on the taxpayers' dime, money that could have gone to pay my aunt Lisa's medical bills due to her inflamed colon?" Keep saying stuff like that and you'll have an army sooner than you think. Remember, manipulation is key.

STEP 2: ARM YOUR ARMY

There are hundreds if not thousands of antique stores in the South that sell firearms. They are all run by old people who can be easily manipulated into selling you their guns for cheap. You want to really tap into the sweet southern charm and speak in euphemisms and metaphors. Say things like, "My oh my! We're living in high cotton today! I swear I'm so hungry I could eat corn through a picket fence! I really need to find a way to get rid of those gators on my farm, but my daddy died in the Iraq War and my momma is blind from staring at the sun waiting for rain to come water our crops! I really need a way to kill these gators." They will then say something like, "My oh my! Sounds like you're in a pickle of a problem! I have some guns in the back I could sell you cheap that you could use to kill those gators!" I'm pretty sure that's what would happen.

NOTE: Whenever you're saying "Yes sir" or "Yes ma'am," make sure you abbreviate. So say: "Yes'm."

STEP 3: MAKE A THREAT

Now that you have arms, gather your army in a big field and set up a camera. Make a video with your army and say, "Hey Mr. President, if you don't step down, then we'll just have to come up to Washington." You can replace Washington with "the Swamp" for dramatic effect. So say, "Hey Mr. President, if you don't step down, we will have to come up to the Swamp and give you a good spanking. You see Leroy here? [Have a really tough-looking guy up front, call him Leroy.] He fought a mule deer with one arm and wrestled it to the ground. You really want him coming up there?"

STEP 4: HYPNOTIZE THE UNITED STATES ARMY

Your new army will now be deemed a "threat" by the government and they will send the US Army to come capture you, at which point you will hypnotize them. See instructions in the next section.

HOW TO HYPNOTIZE THE UNITED STATES ARMY

STEP 1

Print the below image out and hold it in front of a soldier's face.

STEP 2

Say this: "You are getting very sleepy. You are a big strong soldier and you are getting very sleepy. You are feeling regret for the war crimes you've committed. You're *very* sleepy. Go to sleeeeeep (make sure you draw this out). Go to sleeeeeep, my big strong soldier. You are feeling sad about the war crimes. Go to sleeeeeep. You are feeling guilty. You are feeling like you want to join us in our efforts to reclaim this country."

STEP 3

Snap your fingers very quickly and say, "I am now your leader!" At this point the soldier will stand at attention, answering only to you.

STEP 4

Repeat this process individually with each soldier.

Once you have the entire US Army on your side, you pretty much have more power than God himself. Congratulations: you have now successfully taken over the United States government.

10

HOW TO KNOCK OUT A BIRD DRONE'S POWER SUPPLY

7 GREAT CHAINSAWS ON THE MARKET RIGHT NOW

1. Milwaukee M18 FUEL 16 in. 18-Volt Lithium-Ion Battery Brushless Cordless Chainsaw Kit with 12.0 Ah Battery and M18 Rapid Charger ($449)

2. ECHO 20 in. 59.8 cc Gas 2-Stroke Cycle Chainsaw ($449)

As you have learned in the previous section of this book, bird drones charge by perching atop power lines and drawing electricity up through their feet. This is a handy innovation by the engineers who designed the drones: it allows

3. RYOBI ONE+ 18V 10 in. Cordless Battery Chainsaw ($129)

4. DEWALT 20V MAX 12 in. Brushless Cordless Battery Powered Chainsaw Kit with (1) 5 Ah Battery & Charger ($279)

5. RYOBI 40V HP Brushless 14 in. Cordless Battery Chainsaw with 4.0 Ah Battery and Charger ($279)

6. Makita 18-Volt X2 (36V) LXT Lithium-Ion Brushless Cordless 16 in. Electric Chainsaw Kit (4.0 Ah) ($389)

7. Oregon CS1500 Self-Sharpening 15 Amp Corded Electric Chainsaw, 18 in. Bar, Equipped with PowerSharp Saw Chain ($104)

the drones to be self-charging, and allows them to charge in plain sight without anyone knowing. But what if there were suddenly **no more power lines**? That would mean there'd be no way for the drones to charge, and within a few weeks, they would all run out of juice and die.

This would never happen though, because it is illegal to **chop down power lines.** And it would be *very* illegal for someone (say, the leader of a large activism group) to coordinate **a mass effort to chop down all** the power lines in every major city in the United States. I spoke to a lawyer about this, and she said that might even be considered terrorism. So, I wanted to include a brief section in this book where I make it very clear: UNDER NO CIRCUMSTANCES SHOULD YOU **VANDALIZE THE POWER LINES IN YOUR LOCAL CITY IN ANY WAY WHATSOEVER.**

On a completely unrelated note, I have included a brief list of some of my favorite chainsaws currently on the market (pgs. 171–72), in case anyone reading this needs to purchase a chainsaw for at-home tasks such as harvesting firewood or cleaning up a fallen tree in the yard.

HOW TO OPERATE YOUR NEW CHAINSAW

1. **Make sure you're wearing the proper protective equipment**

Before operating the chainsaw, make sure you are wearing protective eye goggles, gloves, and hard-toed boots.

2. **Check your gear**

Make sure the chain on your saw has good tension. If it has more than ¼" of slack, tighten it up a bit (consult your saw's owner's manual for instructions on how to tighten chain).

3. **Power up the saw**

If you're using an electric saw, skip to the next step. If you're using a gas-powered saw, pull the starter rope to power up the saw. You may have to pull the starter rope several times.

4. Prepare to make your cut
Grip the left handle firmly with your left hand. Grip the rear handle firmly with your right hand. Keep your legs a little more than shoulder width apart in order to maintain a stable stance.

5. Make sure there are no witnesses
Quickly survey the area to make sure that no one is watching, especially not the police.

6. Engage the throttle
Press the trigger or throttle. Your chain should now be spinning, and you're ready to make your cut.

7. Make your cut
Release the chain brake and engage the throttle. Make your cut, angling the chainsaw away from you in case it kicks back. Keep the throttle completely engaged until you finish your cut.

8. BAIL
Get out of there as quickly as possible.

HERO
BIRD
TRUTHER

11

A TWO-STEP DEACTIVATION & REPOPULATION PLAN

As you know, our ultimate goal is to deactivate every bird drone nationwide and then reintroduce living birds back into the country so they can begin repopulating. Birds Aren't Real would love to fully replenish the bird population by 2030. Ideally the government would take responsibility for making that happen (since this whole thing is their fault to begin with), but it's looking more and more unlikely that they're ever going to do that. They will probably all go to their graves without ever admitting what they did or doing anything to fix it.

We may have to start taking matters into our own hands.

But can we the people really pull that off? Can regular citizens like you and me band together to destroy billions of bird drones and then replenish the living bird population? Maybe, but it would take a lot of planning and teamwork.

There are some surefire ways to deactivate bird drones, but they're highly illegal and could get you thrown in federal prison (see pgs. 172–73). I don't want to see my fellow Bird Truthers in jail. You can't fight the good fight behind bars. But there is one way to deactivate bird drones I can think of that is not technically illegal. As far as replenishing the live bird population— that part would be tricky. It's illegal to capture live birds and smuggle them across the border. What I'm saying is, there's no *easy* way to pull this off.

But hypothetically it *is* possible. I call this hypothetical plan "Operation: Restock the Flock." Here's how it would work . . .

STEP 1 OF 2: MASS DEACTIVATION OF BIRD DRONES

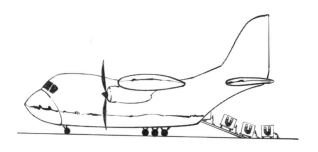

Have you ever held a magnet up to a computer? A powerful enough magnet will completely zap your hard drive and render it useless. The same thing happens when you hold a magnet up to a bird drone. It fries their motherboards and causes them to go haywire and then die soon after that. I have never been able to get close enough to a bird to try it, but other Bird Truthers swear to me that it works. Apparently, there's nothing more beautiful than the sight of a bird drone getting its brain zapped by a magnet.

Zapping every bird drone individually would take so long that it's basically impossible to even imagine. But if we could coordinate a mass effort to "magnetize the sky," bird drones would drop dead by the billions. We could magnetize the sky the same way the CIA poisoned the sky back in 1959: using airplanes.

Imagine how many airplanes there are in the sky at any given moment. Probably thousands. Now imagine there was a Bird Truther (or several) on every single one of those planes, and that each of them checked a luggage bag filled with several very powerful magnets. We could create a magnetic field that covers nearly every square foot of the entire country. Bird drones would begin to fall from the sky by the billions. It would all be over in a single day. It makes me tear up just thinking about it. God, we have to do this.

Coordinating this plan would be very difficult. Even just thinking about the logistics is enough to make my head spin, but I know that the Bird Truther community is made up of highly intelligent people. I know that if we put our heads together, we could pull it off. I for one am ready to get started.

STEP 2 OF 2: REINTRODUCTION OF BIRD SPECIES

The next step of the hypothetical plan would be to start bringing live birds back into the United States. They won't come to the US on their own, because the government has taken measures to scare birds off from ever crossing our border (see pg. 86). The only way they could ever get in is if people started smuggling them in, but like I said, **smuggling birds into the country is illegal**, and we never want to break the law.

That means the only way live birds could ever get back into the US is if people began bringing them in *accidentally*. Imagine you take a nice little vacation to Canada. Perhaps you're enjoying a relaxing camping trip in one of their many wonderful national parks. While you're busy tending to the campfire, some birds fly into your car because it's full of delicious food (bread, fruit, birdseed) and you left all the windows open. Now imagine you didn't even notice they were in there until you drove all the way back to the States. Whoops! There they go, flying off into the lush American forest.

Or, imagine you're on a relaxing beach vacation in Mexico. You bring your suitcase to the beach with you, because you need a way to lug around your towel, sunscreen, etc. And then—oopsie daisy—you leave your suitcase wide open, and also there's 20 lbs. of birdseed in there (you're going to eat it). It's not until you board your plane the next day and return home and open your suitcase that you realize—oh no!—there were several different species of birds in there. That would be terrible, especially if you did this regularly (two or three times a month for several years).

Almost immediately, those birds that you **accidentally** smuggled into the country would begin mating. Within a year, they would establish a thriving population. You'd begin waking up to the sublime sound of birdsong every morning once again, and everything would finally be back to normal.

I know it's emotional to think about this. At this point, you're probably in tears from the overwhelmingly beautiful thought of all the birds being back. I know I am. You should take a minute to pull yourself together before continuing with the book. The next page is intentionally blank. Please rip it out and use it to wipe away your tears and blow your nose before advancing to the next chapter.

12

BIRDS AREN'T REAL: 4 KIDZ

There are certain things that are difficult to explain to children. Sex, tyrannical government overreach, Tower 7, etc. But, it's a parent's job to teach their children about the world. I don't have children myself, but I've often wondered what it would be like if I did—how would I explain bird surveillance to them? It's a grim topic, and explaining it to them could shatter every illusion they have about the world. Children deserve their innocence. At the same time, they also deserve to know that they're the victims of tyrannical government hyper-surveillance.

So, I've decided to write an entire chapter that explains bird surveillance in a fun, child-friendly way. If you are a parent of a child under the age of 14, please show them this chapter immediately.

WARNING:

The following content may be extremely disturbing for children under 14.

DENISE AND THE BIRD

**A children's story by Peter McIndoe and
Connor Gaydos**

Denise was a girl who was like any other
She lived in a house with her father and brother
At school she was friendly and followed the
    trends
But still, the poor girl didn't have any friends

One sunny day as she sipped on her tea
She heard a *chirp chirp*'ing ring out from a tree
Denise went to check on the noise she had
    heard
And there in the treetop she spotted a bird!

The bird flew on down and he told Denise, "Hey"
He said he was lonely and wanted to play
Denise was so happy she shouted with glee
"Finally a friend who will join me for tea!"

From that morning on, they were birds of a
    feather
Who spent every second carousing together
Each day they frolicked around on the lawn
And laughed from the morning right into the
    dawn

But the bird couldn't come with Denise to her
     school
"No pets allowed!" What a terrible rule!
Denise couldn't wait for the school days to end
So she could get home to her feathery friend

One day the bird said, "I think it'd be smart
If I join you at school so we don't have to part
While you sit there learning inside of your class
I'll perch by the window and watch through the
     glass!"

Denise was so happy, she thought it was cool
How her new awesome friend now came with
    her to school!
Then one day the bird said, "I wish that at
    night
I could stay in your room to make sure you
    sleep tight"

So later that evening as everyone slept
She opened her window and in the bird crept
He perched on her dresser and said with a peep
"Now we'll be friends even when we're asleep!"

Denise didn't realize that she and the bird
Were whisp'ring so loud that her father had
    heard
He crawled out of bed and he went to go see
What all of this noisy commotion could be!

He burst in her room and saw something absurd
His daughter Denise had befriended a bird!
He looked at his daughter and that's when he
    said
"Get away from the bird right now. Slowly. Stay
    calm. Listen to me, honey. This bird is not
    your friend. Every bird in the United States
    was systematically killed off by the govern-
    ment and replaced with a series of robotic
    replicas as part of the biggest surveillance
    project in the history of civilization."

Denise was so frightened to find out her friend
Was really a spy, what a terrible end!
Her father said, "Honey, this may cause you
    pain
We have to destroy it by frying its brain"

He got a large magnet and held it up high
And stared the surveillance bird right in its eye
Then held the large magnet right up to its head
It twitched for a minute and then it was dead

No matter your age and no matter your milieu
The birds all around you are spies and can kill
    you
So always remember this lesson you've heard
Birds aren't your friend, so never trust birds

Next time you're playing outside with your pals
Beware of the birds that are in your locale
And if they get close, stay calm and remember:

**You can kill a bird drone by holding a large magnet
up to the side of its head**

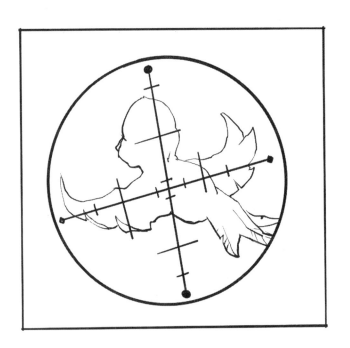

LIL' REBELZ WORD SEARCH

```
Y E M K L W Z E R G X E N O R D D Z A M Q H W
P Z Z M S W S C B I W O N M R A S I D T C G A
D I S C L O S U R E D W N R B H H Z V F I R T
M P O I K E T O T A L I T A R I A N I S M P E
L D Y A S D Z A D N A G A P O R P C N U C I R
W M A K M I C M L I V E F R E E O R D I E W T
R D D I E C A R E S I S T Q K P K I E K H W H
O E N L M O O J R F C P F A V I C I D E Q J E
I A O L O N Z F Z S E I L L L A O J Q H Y G C
U I M E R E O E R C A S S A M Y M Z I X G K O
T R E D Y G N S D Y S T O P I A C A V T P L U
C Z U J H H Y P E R S U R V E I L L A N C E N
H C L F O C M N Y M R D E E P S T A T E Z V T
R A B K L K R W F Z L X W U I A D R I B W S R
D I P A E T V O G W O D A H S N Z G E O H V Y
Z W E T A T S Y N N A N Y V W A R O W M K A O
```

Find the following words in the puzzle.
Words are hidden ↑ ↓ → ← and ↘.

ALL LIES	DYSTOPIA	SHADOW GOVT
AVICIDE	GENOCIDE	TOTALITARIANISM
BIRD	HYPERSURVEILLANCE	WATER THE COUNTRY
BLUE MONDAY	LIVE FREE OR DIE	
CIA KILLED JFK	MASSACRE	
DEEP STATE	MEMORY HOLE	
DISARM NOW	NANNY STATE	
DISCLOSURE	PROPAGANDA	
DRONE	RESIST	

QUIZ

1. You are playing outside with your friends when you notice a bird nearby. What do you do?
   - ☐ Approach it and become its friend
   - ☐ Ignore it and continue playing
   - ☐ Hold a large magnet up to the side of the bird's head

2. The American government
   - ☐ Is my friend
   - ☐ Is not my friend, but it provides me with many important things
   - ☐ Cannot be fixed. It must be torn down and rebuilt from scratch. This is the only way.

3. Birds are
   - ☐ Real
   - ☐ Watching every single thing I do at all times

4. What kind of government do we have?
   - ☐ A democracy
   - ☐ A republic
   - ☐ A bad one

5. In what year did the federal government discontinue the bird surveillance program?
   - ☐ 1970
   - ☐ 1992
   - ☐ There never was a bird surveillance program
   - ☐ They are just getting started

Turn page for answers.

1. You are playing outside with your friends when you notice a bird nearby. What do you do?
   - ☐ Approach it and become its friend
   - ☐ Ignore it and continue playing
   - ☑ Hold a large magnet up to the side of the bird's head

2. The American government
   - ☐ Is my friend
   - ☐ Is not my friend, but it provides me with many important things
   - ☑ Cannot be fixed. It must be torn down and rebuilt from scratch. This is the only way.

3. Birds are
   - ☐ Real
   - ☑ Watching every single thing I do at all times

4. What kind of government do we have?
   - ☐ A democracy
   - ☐ A republic
   - ☑ A bad one

5. In what year did the federal government discontinue the bird surveillance program?
   - ☐ 1970
   - ☐ 1992
   - ☐ There never was a bird surveillance program
   - ☑ They are just getting started

CHILDREN SHOULD STOP READING HERE

13

WHERE ARE WE NOW?

THE CURRENT STATE OF BIRD SURVEILLANCE

It's been over 30 years since the original Birds Aren't Real leader, Clark Griffin, was disappeared by the

Deep State. After that happened, Birds Aren't Real fell into a long "dark age." Without its charismatic leader, the movement fizzled out almost completely. It was the nineties by then, and people were moving on to new causes, like freeing Tibet, fixing the ozone layer, and making the McRib a permanent menu item at McDonald's. That could have been the end of Birds Aren't Real, but it wasn't. In the late 2010s, various pieces of evidence about bird surveillance began showing up online (much of that evidence has been included in this book, including the various classified government documents).

███████ **Media**   November 2, 2015 at 9:32 A.M. ☆ ↩ ⋮

to B.A.R. ▾

●●●

Hey ███████,

Thank you for bringing this to us but we will not be covering this story. We are unable to corroborate any of the evidence you have provided us to show that the government is using bird drones to spy on American citizens.

Respectfully,

███████, Editor
███████ Media

News   November 26, 2015 at 3:27 A.M. ☆ ↩ ⋮

to B.A.R. ▾

•••

,

We're not interested in covering this on ▮▮▮ News.
Nothing you're alleging here seems to be true.

Thank you,

Managing Editor

▮▮▮ News

 Inc.   January 4, 2016 at 7:03 P.M. ☆ ↩ ⋮

to B.A.R. ▾

•••

We are a legitimate news outlet, not a dumping ground
for conspiracy theory nonsense. Please stop emailing
us about birds.

▮▮▮

▮▮▮ Inc.

Suddenly, there was a huge resurgence of interest in bird surveillance. Bird Truthers like me tried to get this earth-shattering information out there to the public as best we could. We reached out to hundreds of news outlets, but we were constantly rebuked and written off as lunatics. To this day, virtually no mainstream media outlets are willing to work with us.

Since mainstream media wouldn't promote our evidence, we began holding rallies in cities throughout America, just like Clark Griffin and the other first-wave activists did back in the seventies. Much like our predecessors, we were not always treated kindly. Passersby would honk their car horns at us, shout insults, throw garbage, and break our signs over their knees. We've been largely written off as raving lunatics, even though we have all the evidence. We are ignored, mocked, censored, and sometimes arrested. Trying to blow this conspiracy wide open often feels like a hopeless battle. Truly we are like the mighty Sisyphus pushing the boulder up the hill. We might never reach the top, but still, we continue to push and push. We will never stop pushing. We will never stop *violating community standards*.

The second wave of Birds Aren't Real activists began filing a series of Freedom of Information Act requests to find out the current state of the bird surveillance program. All our FOIA requests went unanswered. Don't ever make the mistake of thinking the Freedom of Information Act is legitimate. The government does not *have* to surrender any information that they do not want to surrender. Because, after all, what are you going to do about it? What are you going to do when the CIA fails to comply with your orders? Notify the president? Call the police? Tell the mailman!?

It was no surprise that the CIA was unwilling to surrender information. We had no choice but to *take* it. Many of us Birds Aren't Real patriots are just regular people. Honest people, with jobs, families, and responsibilities. But some members of the movement have extraordinary abilities. I am referring to the number of skilled hackers in our ranks.

About a year ago, a skilled hacker and Bird Truther who uses the alias "m4cks" breached a highly secure White House server and managed to leak a trove of classified emails, memos, financial documents, and other incriminating materials going back to 2010. These materials prove, beyond a shadow of a doubt, that bird surveillance is still happening. There was a massive amount of data to sort through. It was hard to work through it all, because it was constantly being wiped from the Internet. The shadow government would have it purged from the web just as quickly as we could re-upload it. To this day, they are still extremely vigilant about purging this information from the Internet. It is almost impossible to find. However, after the initial data dump, I managed to save all the materials onto an encrypted hard drive that I carry with me at all times.

Here are some select highlights, which will show you that bird surveillance is still alive and well today.

EMAIL EXCHANGE BETWEEN CIA DIRECTOR LEON PANETTA, PRESIDENT OF THE UNITED STATES BARACK OBAMA, AND WHITE HOUSE CHIEF OF STAFF RAHM EMANUEL

From: Leon Panetta [mailto: ██████████@cia.gov]

Sent: Monday, May 17, 2010 2:30 PM

To: 'Barack Obama'

Cc: Keith B. Alexander [mailto: ██████████@nsa.gov]

Subject: Update on the bird drone surveillance program

> Mr. President,
>
> Effective immediately the bird drone surveillance program is going to be co-handled by the NSA. I'd like to arrange a time for us to meet with NSA director Keith Alexander and catch him up on the status of the operation.
>
> Thank you,
>
> Leon Panetta
> Central Intelligence Agency Director

From: 'Barack Obama'

Sent: Monday, May 17, 2010 3:14 PM

To: Leon Panetta [mailto: ██████████@cia.gov]

Cc: Keith B. Alexander [mailto: ██████████@nsa.gov],
    Rahm Emanuel [mailto: ██████████@whitehouse.gov]

Subject: Update on the bird drone surveillance program

Sounds good Leon! I'm a littlw swamped this week with Dodd-Frank. And I'm in back-to-back meetings all the way into next week. It never ends!!!

Since I'm so busy I'd like to have you and Keith sit down with my chief of staff Rahm Emanuel. Rah Dog is pretty up to date on the bird surveillance op.

Respectfully,

Barack Obama
President of the United States

From: Leon Panetta [mailto: ██████████@cia.gov]
Sent: Monday, May 17, 2010 3:55 PM
To: 'Barack Obama'
Cc: Keith B. Alexander [mailto: █████████████@nsa.gov],
        Rahm Emanuel [mailto: ████████@whitehouse.gov]
Subject: Update on the bird drone surveillance program

Sounds good. Mr. Emanuel, please let me know when you're available to meet and talk bird surveillance.

Leon Panetta
Central Intelligence Agency Director

From: Rahm Emanuel [mailto: ████████@whitehouse.gov]
Sent: Monday, May 17, 2010 4:00 PM

To: Leon Panetta [mailto: ███████@cia.gov]

Cc: Keith B. Alexander [mailto: ████████@nsa.gov],
'Barack Obama'

Subject: Update on the bird drone surveillance program

Just name the time and place and I'm there. Anything for the bird project. I love what you guys are doing with that whole thing

Rahm "Rah Dog" Emanuel
White House Chief of Staff

From: Leon Panetta [mailto: ███████@cia.gov]

Sent: Monday, May 17, 2010 5:12 PM

To: Rahm Emanuel [mailto: ██████@whitehouse.gov]

Cc: Keith B. Alexander [mailto: ████████@nsa.gov],
'Barack Obama'

Subject: Update on the bird drone surveillance program

Hey Rah Dog (i love that btw lol) would tomorrow at 8am be too early to talk birds?

Leon Panetta
Central Intelligence Agency Director

From: Rahm Emanuel [mailto: ██████@whitehouse.gov]

Sent: Monday, May 17, 2010 5:27 PM

To: Leon Panetta [mailto: ███████@cia.gov]

Cc: Keith B. Alexander [mailto: ███████████@nsa.gov],
   'Barack Obama'
Subject: Update on the bird drone surveillance program

Early bird gets the worm ¯_(ツ)_/¯

Rahm "Rah Dog" Emanuel
White House Chief of Staff

From: Leon Panetta [mailto: ██████████@cia.gov]
Sent: Monday, May 17, 2010 5:40 PM
To: Rahm Emanuel [mailto: ████████@whitehouse.gov]
Cc: Keith B. Alexander [mailto: ███████████@nsa.gov],
   'Barack Obama'
Subject: Update on the bird drone surveillance program

LOL!!!! Ok see you then.

Leon Panetta
Central Intelligence Agency Director

EMAIL EXCHANGE BETWEEN NSA DIRECTOR KEITH B. ALEXANDER AND PRESIDENT OF THE UNITED STATES BARACK OBAMA

From: Keith B. Alexander [mailto: ████████████@nsa.gov]
Sent: Tuesday, May 18, 2010 10:20 AM
To: 'Barack Obama'

Cc: 'Joe Biden'
Subject: Bird mtg

Mr. President,

Me and your chief of staff just met with Leon from CIA on the bird drone program. The short update is that the program continues to be a very effective surveillance measure. But the drones are overdue for maintenance. Most of them have been operating since the 1970s and are starting to break down.

Keith B. Alexander
Director, National Security Agency

From: 'Barack Obama'
Sent: Monday, May 18, 2010 11:11 AM
To: Keith B. Alexander [mailto: ████████████@nsa.gov]
Cc: 'Joe Biden'
Subject: Bird mtg

I will pull some strings at the NIP and see if we can pour more money into bird drone maintenance

Regards,

Barack Obama
President of the United States

From: Keith B. Alexander [mailto: ████████████@nsa.gov]
Sent: Tuesday, May 18, 2010 12:00 PM
To: 'Barack Obama'
Cc: 'Joe Biden'

Subject: Bird mtg

> You da man :)

> Keith B. Alexander
> Director, National Security Agency

From: 'Barack Obama'
Sent: Monday, May 18, 2010 12:33 PM
To: Keith B. Alexander [mailto: ██████████@nsa.gov]
Cc: 'Joe Biden'
Subject: Bird mtg

> Haha true
>   Whatever it takes to keep the operation going. Can't have these bird drones going the way of the dodo!

> Barack Obama
> President of the United States

From: Keith B. Alexander [mailto: ██████████@nsa.gov]
Sent: Tuesday, May 18, 2010 1:44 PM
To: 'Barack Obama'
Cc: 'Joe Biden'
Subject: Bird mtg

> LMAO true. Thanks Barry

> Keith B. Alexander
> Director, National Security Agency

TOP SECRET

NATIONAL SECURITY AGENCY

Funds by Program
FY 2010–2011

Program	2011 Allocated	2011 Requested	2010 Allocated	2010 Requested
Analysis	$500 million	$600 million	$500 million	$550 million
Geospatial Intelligence	$500 million	$650 million	$450 million	$550 million
Data Collection	$1.2 billion	$2.5 billion	$1 billion	$1.7 billion
Cyber Operations	$700 million	$800 million	$675 million	$1 billion
Espionage	$800 million	$800 million	$700 million	$750 million
Counter-intelligence	$1.3 billion	$2 billion	$1.1 billion	$1.7 billion
Human Intelligence Operations	$3.2 billion	$3.5 billion	$2.9 billion	$3.3 billion
Facilities and Logistics	$900 million	$1.5 billion	$840 million	$1.6 billion
Crypto-analysis	$600 million	$600 million	$450 million	$500 million
Bird Surveillance	$4.9 billion	$4.3 billion	$4.7 billion	$4 billion
Total	$14.6 billion	$17.25 billion	$13.32 billion	$15.65 billion

Portion of a classified budget report from the NSA's "black budget." Over $4 billion were allocated to bird drone surveillance in 2011.

EMAIL EXCHANGE BETWEEN UK PRIME MINISTER DAVID CAMERON AND PRESIDENT OF THE UNITED STATES BARACK OBAMA

From: David Cameron [mailto: ███████@gov.uk]
Sent: Wednesday, June 10, 2015 11:27 AM
To: 'Barack Obama'
Subject: Surveillance advice

> Mr. Obama,
>
> How are you, mate? I hope all is well with you and the girls. I'm reaching out for a bit of advice. I'm not sure if you've noticed but the peasants are getting restless over here in the UK. Bloody Brexit talk has got them all worked up. I spoke with the Queen and we agree we need to keep a closer eye on our citizens. Don't want the proles going mental and storming the palace with bloody pitchforks and torches. What are you lot in America doing for domestic surveillance these days?
>
> Respectfully,
> David

From: 'Barack Obama'
Sent: Thursday, June 11, 2015 2:52 PM
To: David Cameron [mailto: ███████@gov.uk]
Subject: Surveillance advice

That's classified lol

But seriously, we use birds. We've been using them since the 1970s.

Barack Obama
President of the United States

From: David Cameron [mailto: ████████@gov.uk]
Sent: Thursday, June 11, 2015 4:22 PM
To: 'Barack Obama'
Subject: Surveillance advice

Eyes in the sky eh? How does that work?
David

From: 'Barack Obama'
Sent: Thursday, June 11, 2015 5:00 PM
To: David Cameron [mailto: ████████@gov.uk]
Subject: Surveillance advice

Basically cia developed a poison to kill off the bird population. They've been replaced with robotic surveillance drones equipped with cameras and microphones. It's been a great way to spy on people.

Barack Obama
President of the United States

From: David Cameron [mailto: ███████@gov.uk]
Sent: Thursday, June 11, 2015 8:58 PM
To: 'Barack Obama'
Subject: Surveillance advice

> Would love to do a similar thing here in the UK. How much
> does an operation like that cost?
> David

From: 'Barack Obama'
Sent: Friday, June 12, 2015 12:24 PM
To: David Cameron [mailto: ███████@gov.uk]
Subject: Surveillance advice

> Ngl it's expensive. It would be hard to do for under $10 bil
>
> Barack Obama
> President of the United States

From: David Cameron [mailto: ███████@gov.uk]
Sent: Friday, June 12, 2015 1:01 PM
To: 'Barack Obama'
Subject: Surveillance advice

> Bloody hell. I'm not sure we've got that kind of money to
> spend on surveillance over here in the UK. We're still using
> CCTV cameras
> David

From: 'Barack Obama'
Sent: Friday, June 12, 2015 2:22 PM
To: David Cameron [mailto: ███████@gov.uk]
Subject: Surveillance advice

> It's worth it to make sure the peasants don't get out of line. If
> your budget is tight I think China managed to do it for pretty
> cheap

> Barack Obama
> President of the United States

From: David Cameron [mailto: ███████@gov.uk]
Sent: Friday, June 12, 2015 3:00 PM
To: 'Barack Obama'
Subject: Surveillance advice

> China is doing bird drones too?
> David

From: 'Barack Obama'
Sent: Friday, June 12, 2015 5:33 PM
To: David Cameron [mailto: ███████@gov.uk]
Subject: Surveillance advice

> Yeah our intelligence agencies have been keeping a close eye
> on China (i don't like the way they've been moving lately tbh)
> and they say President Xi launched a similar bird surveillance

operation in 2014. Pretty sure they stole the idea from us.
Russia is working on it too but so far not successful. They
can't get the bird drones to fly

Barack Obama
President of the United States

From: David Cameron [mailto: ████████@gov.uk]
Sent: Saturday, June 13, 2015 9:30 AM
To: 'Barack Obama'
Subject: Surveillance advice

Can't get the bird drones to fly? They must be using
Ostrich model of bird drone 😁
David

From: 'Barack Obama'
Sent: Saturday, June 13, 2015 10:11 AM
To: David Cameron [mailto: ████████@gov.uk]
Subject: Surveillance advice

Lmaooooo 😴

Barack Obama
President of the United States

From: David Cameron [mailto: ██████████@gov.uk]
Sent: Saturday, June 13, 2015 3:00 PM
To: 'Barack Obama'
Subject: Surveillance advice

> Well anyway, thanks for the insight. Be well mate.
> David

From: 'Barack Obama'
Sent: Saturday, June 13, 2015 7:45 PM
To: David Cameron [mailto: ██████████@gov.uk]
Subject: Surveillance advice

> You too David. And don't forget to "throw another shrimp
> on the barbie!"
>
> Barack Obama
> President of the United States

From: David Cameron [mailto: ██████████@gov.uk]
Sent: Saturday, June 13, 2015 3:00 PM
To: 'Barack Obama'
Subject: Surveillance advice

> That's Australian mate
> David

PHONE CALL BETWEEN PRESIDENT BARACK OBAMA AND SUCCESSOR DONALD TRUMP (NOVEMBER 11TH, 2016)

The following is a transcript of a phone call held on November 11th, 2016—the week Donald Trump won the presidential election. The call was recorded and archived on a White House server, then leaked by m4cks along with the rest of this material.

BARACK OBAMA
Mr. Trump, good morning.

DONALD TRUMP
Good morning, Barry. How are you?

BARACK OBAMA
I'm doing alright. I was just calling to congratulate you on the win. I know we've had our share of differences, but I'd like to officially say, welcome to the White House.

DONALD TRUMP
Well it's really really good, Barry, you know, it's a really good thing I'm getting in there because, I'll tell you what . . . it's a real mess what you got going on. What's happening right now

in the White House and in the
country, people are not happy.
They really aren't, Barack.
Someone needs to get in there
and fix it up, because let me tell
you what people are saying—

BARACK OBAMA

Again, I just wanted to say congratulations.

DONALD TRUMP

Thank you. We ran a fantastic
campaign. A lot of people have
come up to me to tell me, that
was an excellent campaign, what
you did. And some people, they
hate that I won, Barry. They
come up to me and they say,
you never should have won this
election. These are nasty people,
very nasty.

BARACK OBAMA

Right. Before I let you go, have you been briefed
on bird surveillance?

DONALD TRUMP

Bird surveillance, no, I've not
heard of this.

BARACK OBAMA

I'd like you to meet with me and some of the guys at the NSA to brief you on this. This is a very important program, and it's undergoing a lot of changes. It's very important that nothing gets jumbled in the transition.

DONALD TRUMP

Well, I'll tell you what, whatever it is . . . Whatever's going on, we're going to get in there and we're going to take care of everything, me and my people. And I have some excellent people on my side. Mike, of course, Mike Pence, Mike is fantastic. And we—

BARACK OBAMA

Are you available to meet this weekend?

DONALD TRUMP

Well, I'm very busy, Barry. There's a lot to do. We're gonna see what we can do as far as scheduling a meeting.

BARACK OBAMA

There's another issue. There are some so-called "activists" making noise online about bird surveillance. There's been some leaks, and people know about the operation. It's becoming a bit of an open secret. Again, this is a massive surveillance operation. A lot of people have problems with it. The FBI has been monitoring the activists. We're a little concerned this will continue to get out. I'd like you to read the newest threat assessment from the FBI before we meet.

DONALD TRUMP
Well, I'll tell you what I'm going to do, Barry. Send it over, and I'm going to take a look at it. Me and my people, we're going to take a look.

THREAT ASSESSMENT PERSPECTIVE

An investigation into the renewed public interest in anti-bird-surveillance activism.

FBI Academy
Quantico, Virginia

BACKGROUND

From the 1970s through the late 1990s a growing movement of anti-bird-surveillance activists emerged. This movement was sparked by a series of leaks regarding the Central Intelligence Agency's bird surveillance program. By the turn of the century the Federal Bureau of Investigation had deemed the anti-bird-surveillance movement "dead" and no longer considered it a threat to government security. The original activists were thought to have died off, been apprehended, or otherwise been "dealt with."

The Bureau has growing concerns about a resurgence in anti-bird-surveillance activism on the Internet. Classified information regarding the ongoing bird surveillance program has been leaked. Some of these leaked documents date back to the earliest years of the program. Some of the information that has been leaked was never digitized, therefore we believe the hard copies of this information must have been stolen by analog means. It is still unknown if this theft occurred recently or if these materials were stolen in the original wave of anti-bird-surveillance activism and are just now being released online.

INFLUENCE

Renewed interest in bird surveillance began in the late 2010s on various Internet message boards and social media channels. This second wave of activism has been branded the Birds Aren't Real movement. Assessment of the Birds Aren't Real movement's various social media channels shows a 60% spike in interest since 2015. Follower counts and engagement continue to increase at a steady rate.

The Bureau's Cyber Crime division is closely monitoring the Birds Aren't Real movement online. We've confirmed members of the movement have made several attempts at breaching government servers in search of information regarding bird surveillance, but as far as we can determine none of them have been successful. Regardless, classified government information on bird surveillance continues to appear online in various forms. The Bureau is taking the necessary measures to manage these information breaches. Agents are continually having sensitive information wiped. We are actively searching for the source of these leaks.

Birds Aren't Real activism is mostly limited to the Internet but the movement frequently holds live rallies and demonstrations. These live demonstrations have thus far remained nonviolent, and we don't believe they are actively swaying the public.

THREAT LEVEL AND COUNTERMEASURES

A thorough threat assessment by the Bureau shows that the Birds Aren't Real movement is a **MEDIUM CONCERN**. The ongoing leaks are an extreme cause for concern as they highlight some yet-to-be-determined weakness in the federal government's security apparatus. However, the actual effect of these leaks is not an immediate or extreme threat to national security. Opposition to bird surveillance still seems to be limited to a fringe demographic of "conspiracy theorists." An average American would find Birds Aren't Real outlandish, alienating, or otherwise not concerning.

Above: FBI threat assessment

The inherently absurd nature of the bird surveillance program seems to be its greatest asset. The true details of bird surveillance are considered ridiculous by most "normal" Americans and therefore the Birds Aren't Real movement remains a "fringe" cause with a negligible amount of influence and support.

Though we have the capability to take down the Birds Aren't Real movement's various social media channels if we deem it necessary, we have determined it is better to keep them up. The generally unhinged nature of Birds Aren't Real's social media seems to be more alienating than indoctrinating.

We do not believe that supporters of the movement are prone to radical acts of terrorism or general violence. Still the FBI deems it necessary to continue monitoring the movement very closely. "Top members" of the movement limit their communications to encrypted platforms such as Telegram. The Bureau has infiltrated these encrypted chats and is actively monitoring and participating in them.

Above: FBI threat assessment (cont'd)

EMAIL EXCHANGE BETWEEN NSA DIRECTOR PAUL M. NAKASONE AND PRESIDENT OF THE UNITED STATES DONALD TRUMP

From: Paul M. Nakasone [mailto: ██████████@nsa.gov]
Sent: Thursday, January 24, 2019 10:10 AM
To: 'Donald J. Trump'
Subject: Bird drone upgrades

Mr. President,

I just spoke with our engineers from the bird drone project about the proposed upgrades. It will be no problem to upgrade the bird drones with infrared and retinal scanning technology. The only issue will be money. We will need at least 12 billion to make the upgrades.

Paul M. Nakasone

Director, National Security Agency

From: 'Donald J. Trump'
Sent: Thursday, January 24, 2019 1:33 PM
To: Paul M. Nakasone [mailto: ███████████@nsa.gov]
Subject: Bird drone maintenance

> Spoke to Douglas P at the NIP. He tells me they won't allo-
> cate more than 7 billion! WE WILL SEE! I am playing hardball
> for the full 12 billion. Dirty Douglas will FOLD!
> Donald J. Trump

From: Paul M. Nakasone [mailto: ███████████@nsa.gov]
Sent: Thursday, January 24, 2019 2:00 PM
To: 'Donald J. Trump'
Subject: Bird drone maintenance

> Keep me posted
>
> Paul M. Nakasone
> Director, National Security Agency

From: 'Donald J. Trump'
Sent: Friday, January 25, 2019 9:05 AM
To: Paul M. Nakasone [mailto: ███████████@nsa.gov]
Subject: Bird drone maintenance

> As predicted Dirty Douglas at the NIP has agreed to allocate
> the full 12 billion for upgrades to the bird drones. I got him on
> the phone and he folded like a dog! GOOD!!
> Donald J. Trump

From: Paul M. Nakasone [mailto: ███████████@nsa.gov]
Sent: Friday, January 25, 2019 12:22 PM
To: 'Donald J. Trump'
Subject: Bird drone maintenance

> Good We will get started on the upgrades ASAP. We'd like to contract with a company to produce the infrared cameras. We like AMEC Power Instruments as our first option. Will reach out to them
>
> Paul M. Nakasone
> Director, National Security Agency

NATIONAL SECURITY AGENCY

FORT MEADE, MARYLAND

COLLABORATION AGREEMENT BETWEEN AMEC POWER INSTRUMENTS AND THE NATIONAL SECURITY AGENCY

This letter and the attached Term Sheet are made and entered into on FEBRUARY 24th 2019 by and between **THE NATIONAL SECURITY AGENCY** (operating under the authority of the **UNITED STATES DEPARTMENT OF DEFENSE**) and the 'Contractor' (**AMEC POWER INSTRUMENTS**), constituting the entire agreement between both parties regarding the <u>manufacturing of infrared cameras by the Contractor for use by the United States government in domestic surveillance.</u> Any terms used in this Agreement that are not defined clearly herein will be outlined in the attached Term Sheet. Both parties have reached this agreement via friendly consultation and in accordance with all relevant contracting laws of the United States of America. The Contractor hereby acknowledges that their agreement with the National Security Agency to produce infrared cameras requires a level of transparency on behalf of the government that <u>might make the Contractor privy to sensitive, classified government information</u> that is not to be shared under any circumstances. The Contractor understands that sharing any of this information could constitute treason and may result in the maximum penalty (life imprisonment).

    The Contractor hereby makes the commitment to manufacture a minimum of 10 billion infrared cameras that meet the exact specifications outlined in the attached Term Sheet. Failure to deliver on this commitment will require the Contractor to refund all compensation received upon

Above: Contract between the NSA and AMEC Power Instruments to manufacture infrared cameras for bird drones. AMEC did not agree to move forward. The United States has instead contracted with a manufacturer in China.

EMAIL EXCHANGE BETWEEN NSA DIRECTOR PAUL
M. NAKASONE AND PRESIDENT JOSEPH BIDEN

From: Paul M. Nakasone [mailto: ███████████@nsa.gov]
Sent: Monday, February 1, 2021 11:30 AM
To: 'Joseph Biden'
Subject: Bird surveillance check-in

Mr. President,

Me and some people from research and development at the bird surveillance project would like to show you the new bird drone models. They are now equipped with infrared technology and retina scanning. I believe you have been briefed on some of this already. I'd like to discuss some more possible upgrades to implement in the near future. There has been talk of giving the bird drones the ability to intercept phone calls and text messages.

Paul M. Nakasone
Director, National Security Agency

From: 'Joseph Biden'
Sent: Monday, February 1, 2021 1:09 PM
To: Paul M. Nakasone [mailto: ███████████@nsa.gov]
Subject: Bird surveillance check-in

joe biden

From: Paul M. Nakasone [mailto: ██████████@nsa.gov]
Sent: Monday, February 1, 2021 1:37 PM
To: 'Joseph Biden'
Subject: Bird surveillance check-in

   ???

   Please let me know when you are available to meet.

   Paul M. Nakasone
   Director, National Security Agency

From: 'Joseph Biden'
Sent: Tuesday, February 2, 2021 6:36 AM
To: Paul M. Nakasone [mailto: ██████████@nsa.gov]
Subject: Bird surveillance check-in

   ok

From: Paul M. Nakasone [mailto: ██████████@nsa.gov]
Sent: Friday, February 5, 2021 11:45 AM
To: 'Joseph Biden'
Subject: Bird surveillance check-in

   Mr. President,
   I am following up to see when you are available to come see
   the new bird drones. and discuss more possible upgrades

   Paul M. Nakasone
   Director, National Security Agency

From: 'Joseph Biden'
Sent: Friday, February 5, 2021 3:59 PM
To: Paul M. Nakasone [mailto: ████████████@nsa.gov]
Subject: Bird surveillance check-in

> This is joe

From: Paul M. Nakasone [mailto: ████████████@nsa.gov]
Sent: Friday, February 5, 2021 4:33 PM
To: 'Joseph Biden'
Subject: Bird surveillance check-in

> Yes I know. What is your availability this week?
>
> Paul M. Nakasone
> Director, National Security Agency

From: 'Joseph Biden'
Sent: Friday, February 5, 2021 5:00 PM
To: Paul M. Nakasone [mailto: ████████████@nsa.gov]
Subject: Bird surveillance check-in

> What the hell r are you talking about bud

From: Paul M. Nakasone [mailto: ████████████@nsa.gov]
Sent: Friday, February 5, 2021 5:22
To: 'Joseph Biden'
Subject: Bird surveillance check-in

Okay we're just going to go ahead and release the new bird drones.

Paul M. Nakasone
Director, National Security Agency

From: 'Joseph Biden'
Sent: Saturday, February 6, 2021 5:39 AM
To: Paul M. Nakasone [mailto: ██████████@nsa.gov]
Subject: Bird surveillance check-in

ok

PLAN Z

HOW TO BUILD AN UNDERGROUND SOCIETY

In the event that this book fails to take down bird surveillance, and the government finally starts shipping every member of the Birds Aren't Real movement off to Guantanamo Bay once and for all (which they've been trying to do since 1979!), please read this chapter very carefully.

Every great movement must have a "Plan Z." The last resort. Our Plan Z is to move underground and build a new society that is untouched by government surveillance. This would consist of an intricate series of underground tunnels and pipes that we refer to as "The Pipe Dream." Obviously, none of us *want* to go live under the ground, where it's cold and wet and musty, but it's looking more and more inevitable. I've been trying to tell people about bird surveillance for many years now, and most of them continue to just shrug their shoulders and go back to scrolling through TikTok, completely brain-dead. Imagine you're on the *Titanic* trying to warn people, "In two minutes this ship is going to strike an iceberg and sink!" and instead of running to the lifeboats, everyone just shrugs and walks off to the buffet. That's the stage we're close to right now with bird surveillance. An underground society is our lifeboat—the one we're using to sail away from the sinking ship (the sinking ship is America).

This is a comprehensive guide to starting an underground society. Retreating underground and building a whole new world down there will be a difficult process, but if we all work together and stay on the same side, maybe it won't be sad. Anything is better than living in the cruel world of bird drone surveillance, where the smoke from the chimney of Washington, DC, has nearly blocked out all the light.

INTRODUCTION

If you're reading this, that means we have collectively failed. What a nightmare. It's not all bad though, because now we have an opportunity to achieve what we ultimately wanted: a drone-free world. Theoretically bird drones will have a very hard time infiltrating our underground society. And if they do, they should be easy to spot and kill, because there are no trees for them to hide in, or anything like that.

"But what if I don't want to live underground? What if I'm happy enough aboveground, with my house and my career and all my things?" I readily admit that living underground removes you from all aspects of what many consider "a normal life." When you begin telling people that you're going to dig a hole and live in it, they will probably try to talk you out of it. Some of them will laugh at you. They will probably call you things like "moleman" and "dirt eater." Do *not* be swayed.

Noah (from the Bible) was laughed at when he told people he was going to build the Ark of the Covenant. He was mocked and ridiculed, but were they laughing when *they* were drowning and *he* was sitting on the deck with his animals? No. Be like Noah and start digging. Now, let's dig our tunnels!

DIG AN "L-SHAPE" TUNNEL IN YOUR BACKYARD

Feel free to say your "goodbyes" to the outside world before you begin digging. Call your loved ones who're staying aboveground, take one last look at the sun, enjoy a final meal, etc. Go ahead and do this right now if you must . . .

Okay, now gather up your family, go to the backyard, and begin digging a hole. Go *quickly,* because you wasted a lot of time saying your goodbyes.

Begin digging a hole straight down, about 25 feet deep. This is going to be very hard, but you have to push through the pain. Freedom *is* hard. Make sure you really put your back into it. If you have children, you should make them help you dig the hole, because things are going to be really difficult down there and they should start getting used to it.

Once you've gotten 25 feet down into the Earth, begin digging "sideways" to form a tunnel. Make this tunnel about 50 feet long. You should now have an "L" shape in the Earth. This is basically your new driveway.

MAKE A ROOM/HOME

At the end of the tunnel you just dug, dig yourself a "room" about 20 feet by 20 feet. Congratulations: this is your new home. If you have children, they are going to be very upset when you tell them that they live in a big hole now. Make them feel better by assuring them that their lives will be much better underground—anything will be better than the nightmare above. Refer them to the "Birds Aren't Real: 4 Kidz" chapter to remind them of the harsh realities of life on the surface. You may need to reinforce the dangers of bird surveillance multiple times a day so that they remember this is an upgrade. If at any point they begin crying and whining, saying things like

"I miss my friends" or "there's no sun," tell them that this is the price of freedom, and that George Washington is looking down on them from heaven and smiling.

CONNECT WITH OTHERS

Don't worry: you won't get lonely down there. Plan Z is a plan for an underground *society*. The idea is that once you go underground, you'll still easily be able to travel freely and visit your neighbors. All of your fellow subterranean Bird Truthers will just be a tunnel away. To achieve that, we'll need to dig a sprawling system of interconnected tunnels that connect every state.

Once you have established your cave (home), begin digging a new tunnel that begins at your cave and ends directly under your state's capitol building. If every single person who is going along with Plan Z does this, we can create a communal meeting space in each state, which can be accessed by everyone *in* that state.

In order to make underground interstate travel possible, we would then need to create tunnels that connect every single state's communal meeting space with every *other* state's communal meeting space. Once this is accomplished, everyone will be able to travel freely throughout the country. Think of these tunnels as our new highways. You can use them to visit friends and loved ones anywhere in the "country." If this is confusing, please consult the handy tunnel map that I drew myself (see below).

Easy-to-use tunnel map

BUT HOW WILL I LIGHT MY HOME?

That's a great question, and the fact you're asking it shows me you know a thing or two about underground societies. That's good. It *will* be important to find light down there, because naturally it's very dark underground. But do you know what you *can* find underground? I'll give you a hint: the US government spends billions of dollars per year stealing it from other countries. Oil!

That's right—oil, also known as nature's flashlight. As you are digging your underground tunnels you will inevitably stumble upon large deposits of oil. Bring a large bucket to store this oil and use it for lighting your new home. Simply dig a small hole in the floor of your cave, fill it with a small pool of oil, and light it up. You can also use the fire for heating and cooking.

WHERE WILL I FIND FOOD?

Once underground, you will sustain yourself the same way plants and trees do. Think about this: humans eat plants, right? And plants eat nutrients from the soil. By that logic, nothing is stopping us from removing the middleman (plants) and eating soil directly for nutrition. I have personally tested this out. When I was coming up with Plan Z, I ordered some loyal Birds Aren't Real followers see how long they could survive on a dirt diet, and one of them went over 30 days! The dirt diet has been proven to sustain life, and with so much dirt underground, you're literally never going to starve. And before you start complaining and saying, "Boo hoo, I don't want to eat dirt. I want to eat burgers and rotisserie chicken," just think about why you're doing this in the first place. If you want to live a life of gluttony, move to a buffet. If you want to live free, then I'll see you underground. I literally can't make it any simpler than that.

WHERE WILL I GO TO THE BATHROOM?

I don't know.

PARTING WORDS OF WISDOM

You did it. You went underground, far away from the tyrannical eye of the government. It's sad that it had to come to this, but here we are. Here we are in the dirt. It's dark. It's cold. It's not entirely certain this new society won't cave in some day. But you're *free*.

Try to take solace in the fact that this is what the Founding Fathers would have wanted you to do. It's a shame that aboveground, the bad guys are running the show. But down in the dirt, you and your fellow patriots are in control. It will be a simpler, quieter existence, and maybe that's not so bad. Up aboveground, there is constant pressure to accumulate wealth, to climb the ladder, to "make something of yourself." Down in the tunnels, where we patriots roam free and proud, your only responsibility is to survive and be at peace. And who knows? Maybe someday we'll rise again and reclaim the land that was taken from us by the cruel hand of Uncle Sam all those decades ago.

But for now, you're simply free. *Free as a bird.*

TEAR-AWAY FLIERS

For you to hang around town and spread awareness

THE BIRDS ARE NOT WHAT THEY SEEM

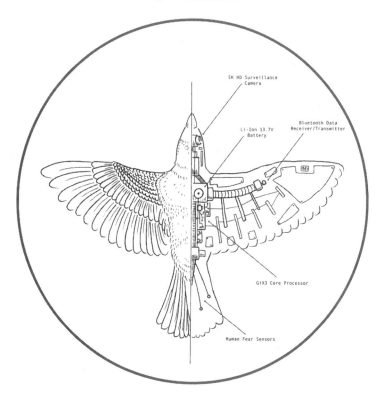

5K HD Surveillance Camera

Li-Ion 13.7V Battery

Bluetooth Data Receiver/Transmitter

G1X3 Core Processor

Human Fear Sensors

**THE GOVERNMENT GENOCIDED ALL BIRDS AND REPLACED THEM WITH
SURVEILLANCE DRONE REPLICAS INDISTINGUISHABLE FROM REAL ANIMALS.
TO LEARN MORE, VISIT BIRDSARENTREAL.COM**

DEMOCRATS ARE LYING TO YOU
REPUBLICANS ARE LYING TO YOU
DEMOCRATS ARE LYING TO YOU
REPUBLICANS ARE LYING TO YOU
DEMOCRATS ARE LYING TO YOU
REPUBLICANS ARE LYING TO YOU
DEMOCRATS ARE LYING TO YOU
REPUBLICANS ARE LYING TO YOU
DEMOCRATS ARE LYING TO YOU
REPUBLICANS ARE LYING TO YOU
DEMOCRATS ARE LYING TO YOU
REPUBLICANS ARE LYING TO YOU
DEMOCRATS ARE LYING TO YOU
REPUBLICANS ARE LYING TO YOU
DEMOCRATS ARE LYING TO YOU
REPUBLICANS ARE LYING TO YOU

BIRDSARENTREAL.COM

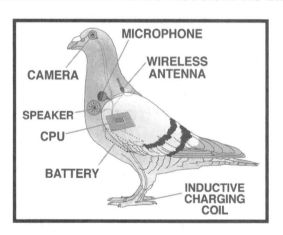

BIRDS AREN'T REAL

Wake Up!

 **=** **GOVERNMENT SURVEILLANCE DRONE**

---

 birdsarentreal.com

ACKNOWLEDGMENTS

In the journey of bringing this book to life, we have been blessed with the support and contributions of so many who have played pivotal roles in our mission. Their dedication, kindness, and belief in this have meant the absolute world to us, and we would like to extend our deepest gratitude to each and every one of them. To Kevin Reilly, Gabrielle Gantz, Stephen Erickson, Susannah Noel, Lena Shekhter, Laura Clark, Lizz Blaise, Omar Chapa, Rob Grom, Guy Oldfield, and the whole team at St. Martin's Press, thank you for helping us get this book out into the world. To Lucas Gardner, this book could not have happened without you. Then there are so many without whom Birds Aren't Real itself would not exist. To Tim Klein, a visionary who saw the light before anyone else did, your early belief in our mission inspired us and set the foundation for all that followed. MK, your generosity in opening up your doors to us when we needed it most will forever be etched in our hearts. To Devin Topf, our movement's official bagpiper, you have graced us with not only your musical talents but also your unwavering love. Your presence in our journey has been a source of inspiration and joy. Taylor, a true hound, your friendship and support while we were in the belly of the beast sustained us during challenging times. To the other Taylor in our lives: you created a bridge to an out-of-character world for us; we love you. Lo/Cal coffee, you were more than just a coffee shop; you were a safe haven where we found solace and inspiration as we finished this book. To Eddie, our true teammate. To Tega, thanks for putting up with us. Thank you to JP, the designer of the bird diagram on the cover, which is actually the first design ever produced for this project. Matt and Bo, you have been our lighthouse many times, guiding us through the darkest of nights with your unwavering support and friendship. Ann Claire, for everything. Eric Francis, for your leadership in leading the state of Missouri to the truth and for always being a true brother of the movement. Your dedication to our cause has been inspiring. Brendan Trachsel, a selfless angel who woke up an entire state and inspired a movement. You are a legend of the brigade, and your impact on our mission is immeasurable. To Claire, for her ministership. To our families, for their boundless love and unwavering support throughout this journey. To Brennan, your lending a hand during a time when it was needed most will never be forgotten. Lauren, without you, without our journey to Memphis that day, this movement would have never come to be. Ethan, your help in Memphis, when the movement was just starting, is something we'll never forget. To Ally, you captured the first moments of the movement's rebirth with your camera, becoming a hero and legend in the entire Birds Aren't Real community. Your eye preserved our history. Ray, the one who made the first sticker, your creative spark ignited our movement. And to our families—thank you for your unwavering love and support, this book is for you. To the countless others who have supported us in various ways, we are forever grateful to all of you, the movement behind the movement.

ABOUT THE AUTHORS

Shannon Moss

Shannon Moss

Connor Gaydos was born in an undisclosed location far from civilization. His father, Clark, was the founder of Birds Aren't Real in the 1970s, and after his disappearance in the mid-1990s, Connor was raised by his uncle Leon. In 2016, Connor ran away from Leon and has since given his entire life to you, the people of America. He knows the risk he's taking by attaching his name to this book, and he asks that if you work at the CIA and are offended by what's inside, you take a few deep breaths and spare his life.

Peter McIndoe is a son, a scholar, and the public information officer for the world-renowned Birds Aren't Real movement. Peter came to the truth in 2017 through a combination of prophetic dreams and independent research. He has spent the past seven years on the road, campaigning in different cities and growing the movement through rallies and grassroots organizing. He's been featured on *60 Minutes* and on the front page of *The New York Times*. Peter's efforts have been credited with growing the movement to millions, and they will possibly save the world. He currently resides in Brooklyn, New York.